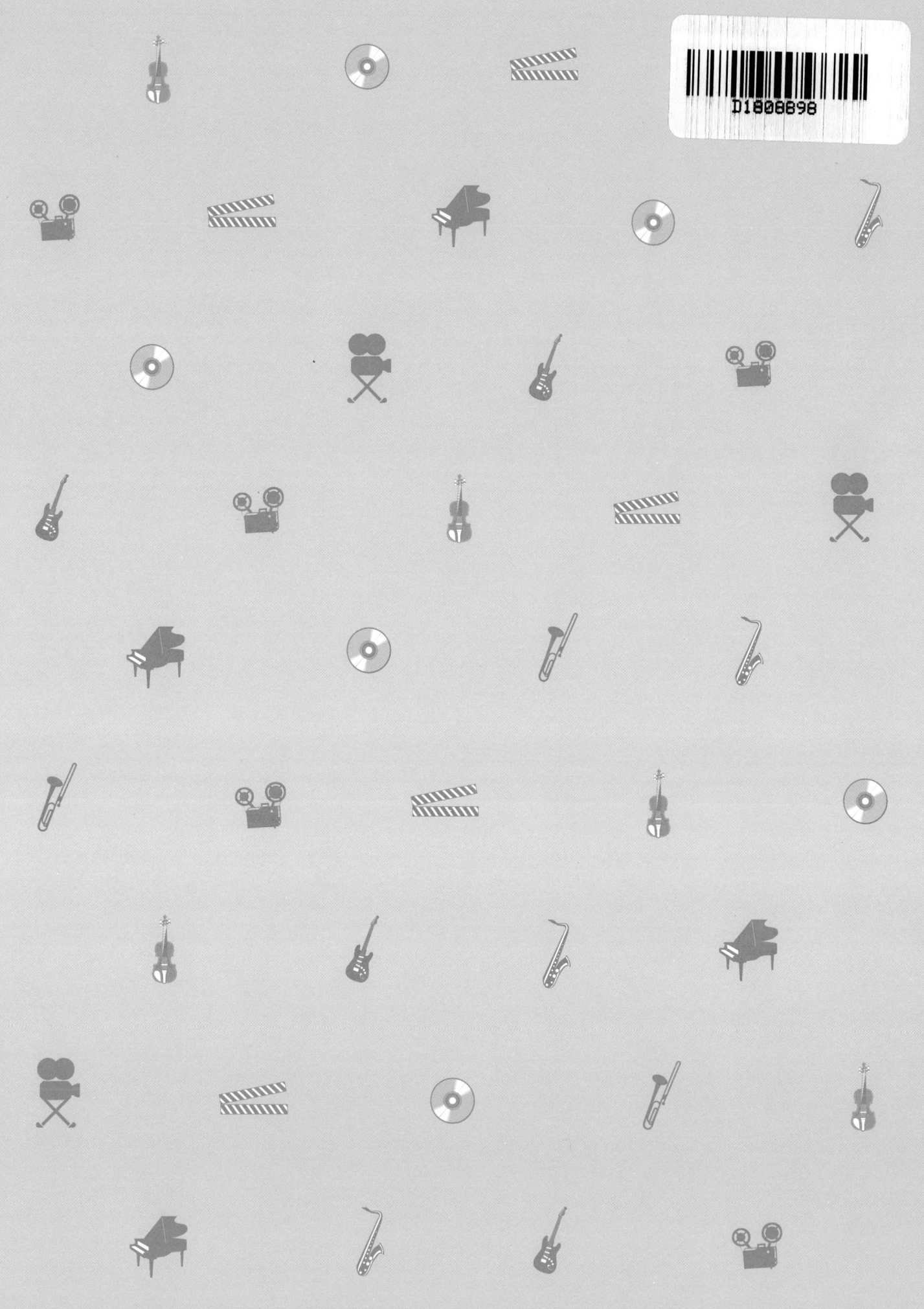

EXPLORING FILM MUSIC

EXPLORING FILM MUSIC

Ian Dorricott
Bernice Allan

The McGraw-Hill Companies, Inc.

Sydney New York San Francisco Auckland
Bangkok Bogotá Caracas Hong Kong
Kuala Lumpur Lisbon London Madrid
Mexico City Milan New Delhi San Juan
Seoul Singapore Taipei Toronto

McGraw·Hill Australia

A Division of The McGraw·Hill Companies

National Library of Australia Cataloguing-in-Publication data:

Dorricott, I. J. (Ian J.)
Exploring film music

ISBN 0 07 470489 3

1. Motion picture music—History and criticism. I. Allan, B. C. (Bernice C.).
II. Title.

781. 542

Published in Australia by
McGraw-Hill Book Company Australia Pty Limited
4 Barcoo Street, Roseville NSW 2069, Australia
Acquisitions Editor: Paul Brock
Production Editors: Sybil Kesteven, Diana Hill
Permissions Editor: Natalie Muir
Designer: Stan Lamond, Lamond Art & Design
Cover Designer: Kerry Harriman, Love of Design
Desktop Publisher: Lamond Art & Design

Cover photograph: Noah Taylor in *Shine*, courtesy of Ronin Films

Printed by Kyodo Printing, Singapore

CONTENTS

To the student vii

THE FUNCTION OF MUSIC IN FILMS 1

SOUNDS AND THEIR QUALITIES 2

'THE CHASE' (Bruce Rowland)—*The Man from Snowy River II* 3

Section 1

EVOKING A TIME AND PLACE 7

'CIRCLE OF LIFE' (Elton John, Tim Rice, arr. Hans Zimmer)—*The Lion King* 8

'MAIN TITLE' (David Byrne)—*The Last Emperor* 12

'RED RIVER CROSSING' (Dmitri Tiomkin)—*Red River* 15

'THE ENTERTAINER' (Scott Joplin, arr. Marvin Hamlisch)—*The Sting* 18

'WALTZ' (Richard Rodney Bennett)—*Murder on the Orient Express* 22

'ON OUR SELECTION' (Peter Best)—*Dad and Dave On Our Selection* 26

'TURKISH MARCH' (Jean-Baptiste Lully)—*Tous les Matins du Monde* 31

'MAIN THEME' (Peter Best)—*The Picture Show Man* 33

'LARA'S THEME' (Maurice Jarre)—*Doctor Zhivago* 33

Section 2

CONVEYING CHARACTER OR IDEAS 35

'THE JAMES BOND THEME' (Monty Norman, arr. John Barry)—*Dr No* 36

'THOSE MAGNIFICENT MEN IN THEIR FLYING MACHINES'
(Ron Goodwin)—*Those Magnificent Men in Their Flying Machines* 40

'THE HEART ASKS PLEASURE FIRST' (Michael Nyman)—*The Piano* 46

'THE RAIDERS MARCH' (John Williams)—*Raiders of the Lost Ark* 50

'MAIN TITLES' (Rachel Portman)—*Emma* 55

'OF FOREIGN LANDS AND PEOPLE'
(Robert Schumann)—*My Brilliant Career* 58

'THE GREMLIN RAG' (Jerry Goldsmith)—*Gremlins* 61

Contents

Section 3   CREATING A MOOD OR ATMOSPHERE   63

'ROCK AROUND THE CLOCK' (Max C. Freeman, Jimmy de Knight,
performed by Bill Haley and the Comets)—*Blackboard Jungle*   65

'BABY ELEPHANT WALK' (Henry Mancini)—*Hatari*   71

'RIVER' AND 'GABRIEL'S OBOE' (Ennio Morricone)—*The Mission*   74

SYMPHONY NO. 25 IN G MINOR, FIRST MOVEMENT, EXCERPT
(Wolfgang Amadeus Mozart)—*Amadeus*   81

THUS SPAKE ZARATHUSTRA, EXCERPT (Richard Strauss), AND
REQUIEM, EXCERPT (György Ligeti)—*2001: A Space Odyssey*   88

'THIS IS A TALE' (Camille Saint-Saëns, arr. Nigel Westlake)—*Babe*   95

'THEME FROM *MISSION: IMPOSSIBLE*' (Lalo Schifrin)—*Mission: Impossible*   101

'THEME FROM *BATMAN*' (Danny Elfman)—*Batman*   103

'PARADE OF THE CHARIOTEERS' (Miklos Rozsa)—*Ben Hur*   103

Section 4   EXPRESSING EMOTIONS   105

'NON NOBIS, DOMINE' (Patrick Doyle)—*Henry V*   107

'THE FIGHTING DONNELLYS' AND 'LEAVING HOME'
(John Williams)—*Far and Away*   111

SYMPHONY NO. 9, FOURTH MOVEMENT, EXCERPT
(Ludwig van Beethoven)—*Immortal Beloved*   118

'PRELUDE' AND 'THE MURDER' (Bernard Herrmann)—*Psycho*   127

'LOVE IS IN THE AIR' (George Young and Harry Vanda)—*Strictly Ballroom*   130

'THEME FROM *SCHINDLER'S LIST*' (John Williams)—*Schindler's List*   134

PIANO CONCERTO NO. 3, FIRST MOVEMENT, EXCERPTS
(Sergei Rachmaninoff)—*Shine*   138

'ANVIL OF CROM' (Basil Poledouris)—*Conan the Barbarian*   141

APPENDIXES

    Solfa hand signs   143

    Major and minor key signatures   144

    Recorder fingering chart   145

    Guitar chord chart   146

    Practical instrument ranges   147

Glossary   148

Acknowledgments   151

TO THE STUDENT

The aim of *Exploring Film Music* is to develop and extend the listening, writing and performing skills you have gained from your previous study of music. We shall be investigating pieces in many different styles taken from a wide range of films, which have been chosen for their appeal and, in many cases, for their 'classic' status. All of the essential musical elements will be discovered, including rhythm, melody, harmony, timbre, texture, tonality and form.

The text can be used in a number of different ways, depending on your year level and your degree of experience. For first-year elective music students *Exploring Film Music* can form the basis of a sequenced course of study; for those of a higher level, sections of the text can provide shorter units of study; for advanced students individual works can be selected from each of the four sections to form the basis of an interesting film music unit.

Great emphasis is placed on practical music making, with a large number of songs, instrumental arrangements and other performance activities provided in the accompanying *Score Book*. In addition, your text contains numerous themes and related melodies for you to play on a melody instrument. This practical approach is not only the best way to learn music, it is also fun.

THE FUNCTION OF MUSIC IN FILMS

Which of you, on hearing the first sinister, low-pitched notes of the theme from *Jaws*, does not instantly form a mental picture of the great monster of the deep? Can you imagine the shark moving in to attack without the accompanying music which intensifies the horror and sheer terror as it becomes louder, higher pitched and thicker in texture? In scenes like this it is the music that is the communicating link between the visual image on the screen and the audience.

In the days of the silent movies, in the early decades of the twentieth century, musical accompaniment to set the scene, define the characters, or heighten the tension was provided by piano, organ or even by an orchestra. This music was either improvised or adapted from existing composed pieces. Since the 1930s film composers have been conveying ideas to the audience by means of specially composed music, usually written for orchestra. The musical score can fulfil a number of different functions, such as:

- to depict the time and place of the setting;
- to convey character or ideas;
- to highlight the mood or atmosphere;
- to communicate to the audience the changing emotions of the characters, their innermost thoughts and their changing states of mind.

In this book we shall be investigating some of these functions, using musical examples by leading film composers, both past and present. Along the way we shall also be discussing the basic elements of music and how composers manipulate them for dramatic effect.

🔺 The great silent movie star Charlie Chaplin

'It is the film composer's job to read the film for its intentions and make what the film's about enjoyable, thrilling, accessible and touching. He's the last person in the process who can react to the picture and put an interpretation on it.'

GEORGE FENTON, COMPOSER FOR *CRY FREEDOM, GANDHI, DANGEROUS LIAISONS* AND *THE FISHER KING*

SOUNDS AND THEIR QUALITIES

No matter what kind of music composers write, they are simply manipulating sounds within silence. The kinds of sounds they choose are determined by how the 'qualities' or characteristics of the sounds—their **pitch** (highness or lowness), **volume** (loudness or softness), **duration** (length) and **timbre** (tone colour)—fulfil a function or suit a dramatic purpose. Film composers in particular must choose their sound qualities with care so that the full impact of a visual scene can be brought out in the accompanying music or **score**. As an example, let us listen to the music of the chase scene from the Australian film *The Man from Snowy River II*.

▲ *The excitement of the galloping horses in the movie* The Man from Snowy River II *is portrayed in the sounds used by composer Bruce Rowland*

'THE CHASE' (BRUCE ROWLAND)

from *THE MAN FROM SNOWY RIVER II*

The 1988 film *The Man from Snowy River II*, the sequel to the internationally acclaimed *The Man from Snowy River*, continues the story of Jim Craig, his endeavours to make enough money to be able to marry his sweetheart Jessica and his struggles with his rival Alistair Patton. As in the first film, the music, by award-winning composer Bruce Rowland, plays an important part in helping to create the excitement of the spectacular action sequences. Rowland uses the four qualities of musical sounds as well as **tempo** (the speed of the music) and **texture** (the combination of sounds in ever-changing densities, sometimes thick, sometimes thin) for his orchestral music to portray each group of horsemen, to picture the different scenes and to create the mood.

There are five main **themes, or** musical ideas, used in the final chase scene, which are given on page 4. Theme A is the heroes' theme and is associated with Jim and his friends. Theme B is used for Patton and his gang. Theme C, the chase theme from *The Man from Snowy River*, heightens the excitement of the chase. Theme D is used for the horses in slow motion; and theme E, a variation on the main theme from the first film, depicts the final victory.

Listen to the themes played to you by your teacher so that you will recognise them when they occur in the chase scene. View the excerpt from *The Man from Snowy River II*, then complete the 'Listening activity' top right as you view it again.

 ## Listening activity

Listen to the music in the chase scene from *The Man from Snowy River II* taking particular notice of how it is used in the various parts of the scene listed below. For each part identify the theme used (theme A, B, and so on), and describe the characteristics of the music (such as pitch, volume, duration, timbre, tempo and texture) and the mood created by the music.

Scene outline

1. Jim begins his chase after the horse thieves.
2. Jim is joined by Jessica, her father and the mountain men.
3. Patton and his gang leave their overnight camp with the stolen horses.
4. Chase continues: scenes of Jim and friends alternate with scenes of Patton and his gang.
5. Slow-motion shots of horses crossing a stream followed by the riders.
6. Chase continues till Patton and his gang are surrounded.

THE BASIC PLOT
of *The Man from Snowy River II*

The scene is the Snowy River high country in the 1880s. Jim Craig (Tom Burlinson) returns from the plains with a herd of breeding horses and intends to ask for the hand of his sweetheart, Jessica Harrison (Sigrid Thornton), in marriage. He learns that Jessica's father is busily arranging a marriage for her with Alistair Patton (Nicholas Eadie), son of the local influential banker. When Harrison forbids Jessica from talking to Jim she angrily rides off to stay with him in his mountain hut. Alistair gathers a gang of rustlers together and they steal Jim's horses, driving them towards the Victorian border. Jim follows on his wild black stallion and is joined by Jessica, her father and the mountain men. The rustlers are cornered, the horses are recaptured and Jim's life is saved by his black stallion.

Theme A

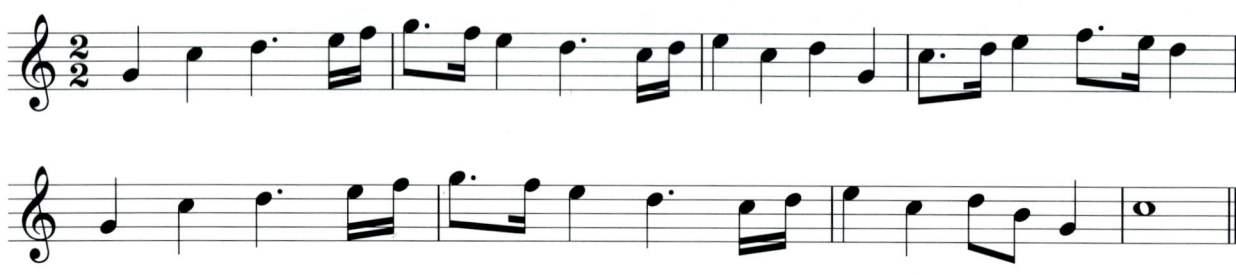

Theme B

Theme C

Theme D

Theme E

Practical activities

1. Play the main theme from *The Man from Snowy River* on page 5.
2. Working in small groups, devise a short film scene such as a car chase or an attack by an alien from outer space. Using available instruments improvise mood music that would be suitable to accompany your scene. Consider the four basic qualities of sounds as well as tempo and texture in your improvisation.

COMPOSER PROFILE

Australian composer Bruce Rowland, born in 1942, began his career as a back-up musician with such stars as the Bee Gees, Olivia Newton-John, Peter Allen and Johnny O'Keefe. His first great success came in 1982 with the score for *The Man from Snowy River*, for which he won an Australian Film Institute award and which is the largest selling film score in Australia. Rowland also won AFI awards for *Phar Lap* (1983) and *Rebel* (1985). His other film scores include *Lightning Jack* (1994) and *Northstar* (1986). He has written many scores for television productions, including *All the Rivers Run* and *Anzacs*, and was the composer of the opening music for Expo 88.

A MOVIE THEME TO PLAY

The 1982 film *The Man from Snowy River* was one of the most successful Australian movies ever produced. Not only did the composer win an Australian Film Institute Award and an APRA Award for the Best Film Score but the album sales achieved double platinum. The main theme from *The Man from Snowy River* is a simple, tuneful melody which is referred to in theme E from the chase scene in the sequel.

Theme from The Man from Snowy River

Bruce Rowland

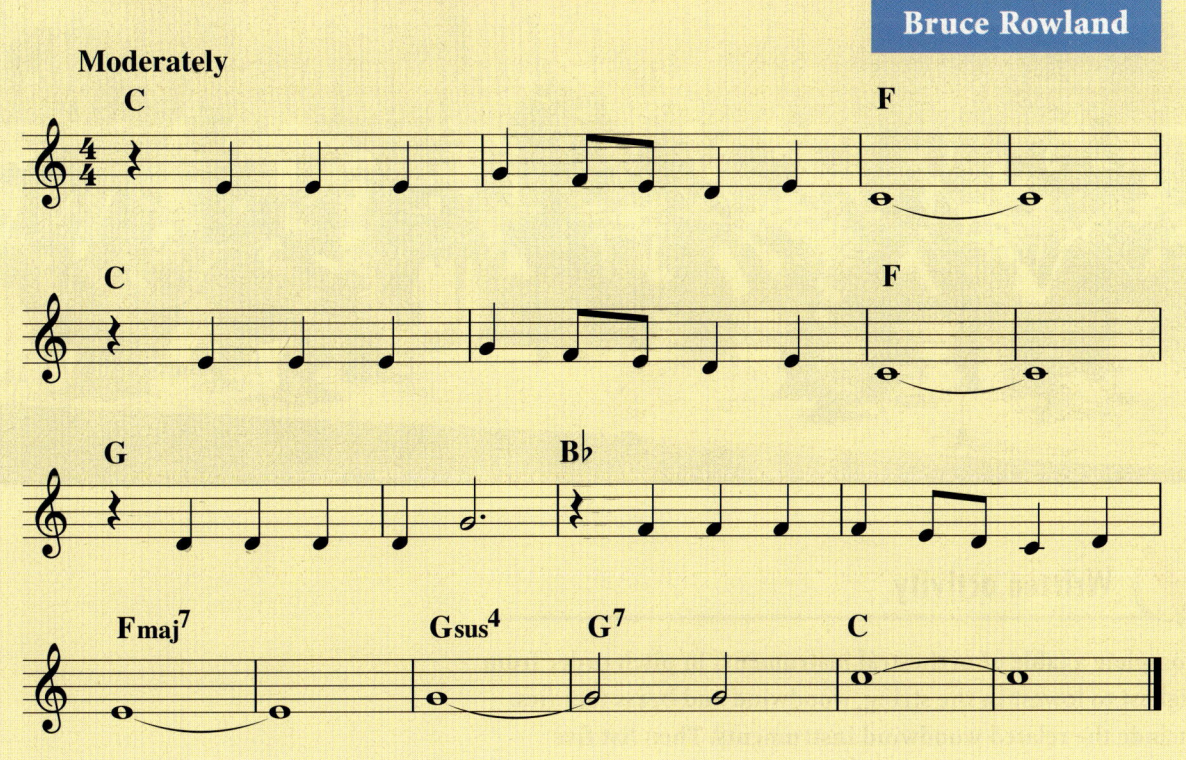

THE ORCHESTRA

Although any instrument or any group of instruments can be used in a film score, the source of sounds for most scores is the symphony orchestra. This is no doubt due to the sheer size of the orchestra—over 90 players—and the fact that it can produce such an enormous range of sounds which can effectively illustrate the range of emotions likely to be experienced in a film. Orchestras were used exclusively in the 1930s and 1940s when emotional scores, written by composers schooled in the European orchestral tradition, were the order of the day. The 1950s saw the introduction of jazz-influenced scores which required smaller, less expensive orchestration, while rock music was popular in the 1960s. However, composers still used orchestras for epic films such as *Lawrence of Arabia* (1962). Since the 1970s orchestras have been widely used, especially for 'blockbusters' such as *Star Wars* (1977) and *Batman* (1989), where a spectacular sound is required for spectacular visuals.

To fully appreciate the many orchestral pieces in this book it is recommended that you first investigate the make-up of the orchestra: the various 'families', the instruments in these families and the pitch and timbre of their sounds. Your teacher will play you examples of the sounds of various orchestral instruments which you should try to remember. Take note especially of those instruments whose sounds are striking or unusual as these will no doubt feature in the scores to be discussed.

▼ *A symphony orchestra*

 Written activity

Complete a table of orchestral instruments in pitch order from highest to lowest in the string, woodwind and brass families. Include the related woodwind instruments. Then list five tuned and four untuned percussion instruments.

▶ *Mel Gibson in a scene from Braveheart (1995). Composer James Horner evokes a sense of ancient Scotland through the use of Celtic instruments and musical elements.*

EVOKING A TIME AND PLACE

A term frequently used to describe an effective film score is the word 'evocative'. This means that the music 'evokes' or 'calls up' for the viewer a feeling, a memory or a sense of time and place that help to set the film in a particular historical era in an identifiable country or location. To achieve a sense of time and place, a composer incorporates elements of the music associated with the setting, such as the rhythms, melodies and instruments, and, if it is vocal music, the language or accent. To illustrate this, let us examine a song from the 1994 animated film *The Lion King*.

'CIRCLE OF LIFE'

from *THE LION KING*

(Music by ELTON JOHN, lyrics by TIM RICE, arranged by HANS ZIMMER)

Walt Disney Pictures' *The Lion King* was the studio's thirty-second animated feature and the biggest grossing film of 1994. Set in darkest Africa, it tells the story of the young lion cub Simba who loses his royal birthright to an evil uncle, only to regain it after a series of dramatic and turbulent events. Featuring a cast of colourful characters, some evil and some comical, *The Lion King* is noteworthy for its brilliant animation, its powerful African-influenced musical score by Hans Zimmer, and five memorable songs by rock singer–songwriter Elton John and lyricist Tim Rice.

The inspiring and emotional 'Circle of Life' is heard at the beginning of *The Lion King*, when the whole animal kingdom is gathered to pay homage to the lion king Mufasa. It immediately suggests the continent of Africa by the use of the dark-timbered, unaccompanied African voice singing Zulu lyrics. (The use of an African language, which is incomprehensible to many of us, gives the continent a mysterious, remote quality.) The solo singer is answered by a group (**call-and-response**), after which begins a web of **ostinatos** (repetitive patterns) chanted by voices and played on African percussion instruments. Thus within the very first moments we hear the main elements of African music: call-and-response, chants, ostinatos, **polyrhythms** (different rhythms heard simultaneously), and the use of traditional percussion instruments. These elements, skilfully woven into the musical setting of 'Circle of Life' by arranger Hans Zimmer, underlie the whole song and help evoke the feeling of untamed Africa.

Listen to 'Circle of Life' following the 'Listening outline' below and noting the African elements mentioned above.

THE BASIC PLOT
of *The Lion King*

Simba the lion prince is born in Africa to the great King Mufasa, thereby making the King's brother Scar second in line to the throne. The evil Scar plots with the hyenas to kill Mufasa and Prince Simba so as to make himself king. The King is killed and Simba is led to believe by Scar that it was his fault, and so flees the kingdom in shame. After years of exile he is persuaded to return home to overthrow the usurper and claim the kingdom as his own, thus completing the 'Circle of Life'.

Listening outline

Introduction ...	Call-and-response between African soloist and group; rhythmic vocal chant; African percussion instruments playing ostinatos, creating polyrhythms with the voices
Verse 1	Solo singer accompanied by a vocal chant, long-note vocal backing and percussion ostinatos
Verse 2	Similar to Verse 1 but thicker texture with added voices
Chorus	Thicker texture again with added drum kit, becoming louder
Verse 3	Panpipe solo accompanied by vocal chant, electric keyboard and percussion instruments; thin texture, soft volume
Verse 4	Similar to Verse 3, becoming gradually louder
Chorus	

 **Aural activity**

Notate the rhythm of the vocal chant that is repeated throughout 'Circle of Life'.

COMPOSER PROFILE

Hans Zimmer, born in Germany in 1957, is one of the most successful of the younger generation of composers and arrangers for films today. He is a pioneer in the use of digital synthesisers integrated with advanced computer technology and electronic keyboards; he also composes music for the traditional orchestra. Zimmer has written music for dozens of films, including *Driving Miss Daisy*, *Thelma and Louise*, *The Power of One* and *Backdraft*, as well as *The Lion King* for which he composed the instrumental music and arranged the Elton John/Tim Rice songs. African-born singer/arranger Lebo M., who wrote the Zulu lyrics in 'Circle of Life' and in the other songs in *The Lion King*, assisted Zimmer with the vocal arrangements. The pair recruited and recorded singers in Los Angeles, London and South Africa to produce the choral sounds that give the songs their distinctively African flavour.

'I think music is a great way of telling a story, especially where words don't quite reach you. Emotions are universal and music is the universal language.'
HANS ZIMMER

 *African drums*

AFRICAN MUSIC

Traditional African music is used as a way of preserving culture. Because many African tribes do not have a written language, stories of past events—as well as moral teachings and religious beliefs—are passed down from one generation to another through songs and dances. ('Circle of Life', which explores the mystical belief in the regenerating power of nature, should be understood in this light.) Other features of African music include the importance of rhythm, the use of repetition as a means of structuring a piece, the simultaneous playing or singing of different musical ideas by performers who frequently begin at different times, call-and-response, and the use of unchanging tempos.

Percussion instruments predominate in African music because the most important element is rhythm. These instruments include rattles, shakers and drums in many shapes and sizes. Drums can be made out of hollowed-out objects such as logs, clay pots or gourds (the dried shells of melon-like fruits), the tops of which are covered with animal skins, and some can be tuned to imitate the pitch patterns of speech. A tuned percussion instrument used in 'Circle of Life' is the *balafon*, a primitive xylophone with gourd resonators under the wooden bars to amplify the sounds. Wind instruments include horns, made from animal horns or tusks, and whistles and flutes made from wood, bamboo or horn. (The flute-like instrument featured in 'Circle of Life' is actually a panpipe. Although it is a South American instrument, the panpipe has a pure, mystical tone which helps evoke the primitive feeling of the song.)

'Disney storytelling magic meets the musical powers of 1992 Academy Award-winning lyricist Tim Rice, Grammy Award-winning writer and performer Elton John, and renowned composer Hans Zimmer in the original motion picture soundtrack for Walt Disney Pictures' animated masterpiece, *The Lion King*. Weaving the rhythms and sounds of Africa into its captivating songs and evocative score, this soundtrack creates a sweeping musical landscape you'll never forget.'

(FROM THE CD COVER NOTES OF *THE LION KING* ORIGINAL MOTION PICTURE SOUNDTRACK)

WRITING A SIMPLE PERCUSSION SCORE

When writing for a group of instruments there are certain basic guidelines that need to be followed so that the score can easily be read. To understand these guidelines let us study the 'Sample percussion score' given below. You will notice that:

1. each instrument has its own staff;
2. the staves are joined by a 'staff line' on the left-hand side;
3. a brace is placed to the left of the staff line;
4. the instrument name is written to the left of the corresponding staff;
5. the time signatures on each staff are directly in line;
6. bar lines are drawn through all staves (showing that the instruments are all the same type);
7. beats and subdivisions of the beats are directly in line throughout all staves;
8. note stems are joined according to the value of the beat.

Note that there are no clefs because all of these instruments are untuned percussion.

 Practical activities

1. Improvise ostinato patterns to accompany 'Circle of Life'.
2. In small groups create a poly-rhythmic composition by improvising appropriate ostinato patterns on available untuned percussion instruments. Play your composition to the rest of the class.
3. Perform the 'Polyrhythmic percussion score' in the *Score Book*.
4. Devise call-and-response phrases, either vocal or instrumental, and perform them to accompanying percussion ostinatos.

 Aural activity

Notate the rhythmic ostinatos played by your teacher.

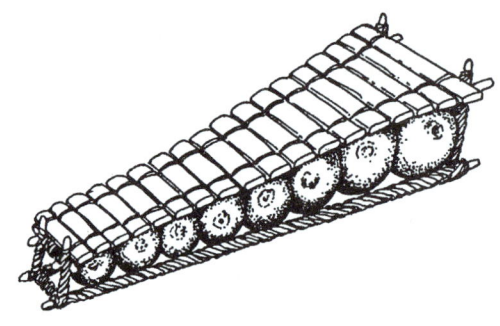

Balafon (see page 9)

Sample percussion score

Shakers

Cowbell

Drum

Written activities

1. Rewrite the percussion score below, correctly aligning the beats and subdivisions of the beats.

2. Write a percussion score for drum, cowbell and claves, setting out the score according to the guidelines on page 10.

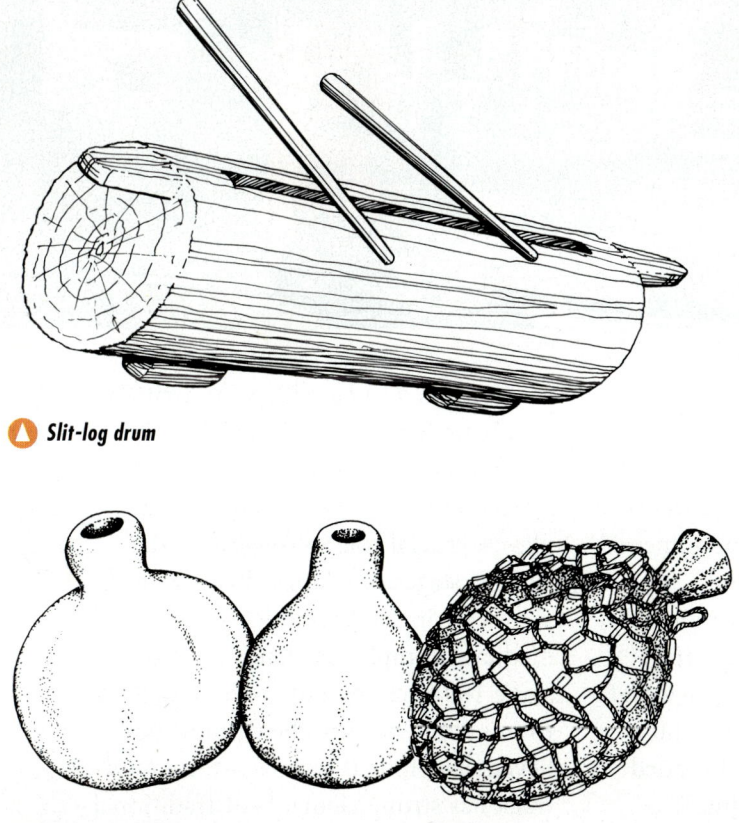

▲ Slit-log drum

▲ Gourds and rattle

'MAIN TITLE' (DAVID BYRNE)

from *THE LAST EMPEROR*

The epic 1987 film, *The Last Emperor*, has been described as 'a magnificent journey to another time and place'. The film deals with events in China between 1905 and 1959—an era of monumental change in Chinese history. First, the Manchu Dynasty, an ancient monarchy, was replaced by a republic in 1912; then in 1931 the Japanese invaded and gradually overran the country; and finally in 1949 Mao Zedong founded the People's Republic of China. *The Last Emperor*, which received nine Academy Awards, including one for Best Original Score, is a biography of Pu Yi (the 'last Emperor'), whose life is shaped by the dramatic events taking place around him.

Music in *The Last Emperor*, written chiefly by Japanese rock star Ryuichi Sakamoto and by David Byrne (of the American rock group Talking Heads), plays a crucial role in suggesting the various stages of Chinese history. In the scenes set in the Forbidden City—a vast medieval complex in Beijing covering some 100 hectares and containing 9999 rooms (only heaven, the Chinese believed, had 10 000 rooms)—the soundtrack has strong elements of traditional Chinese folk music symbolising the old order, feudalism, in which the peasant society was ruled by the all-powerful, god-like Emperor. In the scenes set in the 1930s and 1940s the music reflects the influences of popular Western culture,

▲ *The three-year-old Pu Yi on the steps of his palace in the Forbidden City in* The Last Emperor

and in the post-war communist era revolutionary songs, which were used for propaganda purposes, are featured.

The 'Main Title' music by David Byrne, though played on a Fairlight synthesiser, evokes the sounds and musical elements of traditional Chinese music. The underlying polyrhythmic percussion accompaniment suggests the wooden clappers, drums, gongs and cymbals frequently used to keep the beat in traditional operas and ensembles. The instrument playing the melody is a synthesised *erhu*, one of the most widely used bowed instruments in China. (The erhu has two strings, and the hair of the bow passes between them. The sound box is covered by snake skin and this gives the instrument its distinctive tone colour.) The erhu melody of the 'Main Title' is based on the notes of the **pentatonic scale**, a five-note scale which features in much traditional Chinese music (see below right).

Play the melody of the 'Main Title' from *The Last Emperor* given in the *Score Book* and then listen to the music, following the 'Listening outline'.

THE BASIC PLOT
of *The Last Emperor*

The story of Pu Yi's eventful life is told in flashback/flashforward style and traces his story from his coronation at the age of three, when he is imprisoned in the magnificent Forbidden City, to his abdication at age seven, his dethronement and then re-enthronement as a puppet-king in Japanese-occupied Manchuria, his imprisonment by the Russians, his ten-year 're-education' by the communist Chinese in a war-criminals' prison and, from 1959 when he was pardoned, his final years as a gardener in the Beijing Botanical Gardens.

Listening outline

Introduction ... Ostinato on drums with added clappers and shakers; pentatonic, semiquaver ostinato on xylophone; both ostinatos continue throughout with slight variations; end marked by a cymbal (which also marks the end of subsequent sections)

A .... Erhu melody accompanied by sparse string chords which continue throughout

A¹ .... Similar to A but harmonised at start

B .... Erhu melody

A² .... Similar to A¹ with extended harmonisation

A³ .... Similar to A²

B¹ .... Similar to B with extended backing harmonies

C .... Two new melodies, the lower one an ostinato played on zither (*ch'in* or *cheng*), and the higher one a variation of the A melody with glissandos

A⁴ .... Similar to A² with zither ostinato and differently pitched gongs

B² .... Similar to B¹ with zither ostinato and gongs

Coda .... Based on opening phrase of A with added gongs

The pentatonic scale

The melodies used in the 'Main Title' from *The Last Emperor* are based on an arrangement of five notes called the pentatonic scale. (A **scale** is a series of notes arranged in pitch order.) The notes of this scale can be sung to the solfa syllables doh, re, mi, soh and la. Three different pentatonic scales are given below with doh as C, F and G respectively.

The pentatonic scale is not only to be heard in Chinese music; it is widely used in folk songs all around the world, in such countries as Japan, France, England, Scotland, Ireland, the United States of America and Canada, and in African nations. It is also a feature of many **spirituals**, the religious songs of the African-Americans whose ancestors were transported to North America as slaves. A selection of pentatonic folk songs is given in the *Score Book*.

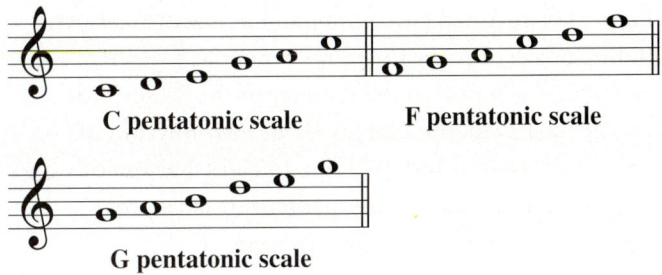

C pentatonic scale   F pentatonic scale

G pentatonic scale

CHINESE MUSIC

Music and the performing arts are thought to have been used in China for festivals and ceremonies and as an accompaniment to ritual at the Chinese court for nearly 5000 years. For the past 2000 years the music has been enriched by absorbing influences from other countries such as India, Persia (Iran) and Mongolia.

The important elements of Chinese music are melody and timbre. The melodies, usually just two or three phrases, are often based on the five-note pentatonic scale given on page 13 and accompanied by percussion instruments providing free rhythmic backgrounds. Interest is created by a variety of tone colours as a number of instruments play the same melody, some decorating it with small variations.

The main instruments belong to eight categories: metal, stone, clay, skin, silk, wood, gourd and bamboo. In addition to the erhu and percussion instruments mentioned earlier, important Chinese instruments include the *ch'in* and *cheng* (types of zither), the *p'ip'a* (a large pear-shaped lute), the *san sien* (a long-necked square-shaped lute), the *yueh ch'in* (a moon-shaped guitar), the *ti tse* (a bamboo flute) and the *sheng* (a type of mouth organ with 17 bamboo pipes).

 Chinese musicians playing a ch'in and a sheng

 Practical activities

1. Improvise ostinato patterns on tuned and untuned percussion instruments to accompany the 'Main Title' from *The Last Emperor*. (Use the G pentatonic scale on your tuned percussion instruments.)
2. Play 'Sample pentatonic score' in the *Score Book* on tuned and untuned percussion instruments. The melody lines are based on the F pentatonic scale.
3. Working in groups, improvise your own pentatonic ostinato patterns and combine these with improvised ostinatos for untuned percussion instruments.
4. Sing and play the pentatonic folk songs in the *Score Book*.
5. Working in groups, devise a pentatonic melody, four to eight bars long and write it out. Work out at least two ostinatos for untuned percussion and at least two short pentatonic ostinatos for tuned instruments. Organise a piece for performance in the manner of the 'Main Title' from *The Last Emperor*. Start with an introduction of untuned percussion; add the four- to eight-bar melody and then gradually add your other pentatonic ostinatos, varying these slightly from time to time.

Written activities

1. Write the ostinato patterns that you improvised in 'Practical activity' no. 3. Set out your patterns according to the guidelines on page 10. Use a clef for the pentatonic patterns. Join the bar lines of the tuned instruments and the bar lines of the untuned instruments, as in 'Sample pentatonic score' in the *Score Book*.
2. Compose four pentatonic melodies. Sing or play them with others written by your classmates. (You can combine any number of these melodies, provided they are based on the same pentatonic scale.)
3. Write a song (with lyrics) based on the pentatonic scale.

 Aural activity

Notate pentatonic melodies played by your teacher.

'RED RIVER CROSSING' (DMITRI TIOMKIN)

from *RED RIVER*

▲ *The cattle crossing scene in* **Red River**

Red River is ranked as one of the greatest American westerns of all time. The epic 1948 film, set in the mid-nineteenth century, tells of the men who made the first cattle drive up the Chisholm Trail from Texas to Kansas under the leadership of Tom Dunson, played by the greatest western actor of all, John Wayne. To match the grandeur and spectacle of the images, director Howard Hawks called on Dmitri Tiomkin, one of the leading Hollywood composers of the time, to compose the music. The resulting score, one of many Tiomkin wrote for westerns, reflects his view of the vastness, grandeur, beauty, primitiveness, innocence and romance of the American West. (Tiomkin was born in the Ukraine, also a vast, open and in some parts primitive country, the homeland of the rugged, horse-riding Cossacks, who were in many ways similar to the American cowboys. This may explain why his music is so in tune with the subject matter.)

Like many composers of the time, Tiomkin wrote musical themes—some short phrases, some whole melodies and others whole pieces—associated with a person, place, object, animal or idea. This process has become stock-in-trade for film composers. The themes used throughout a film can also undergo variation and transformation, reflecting changes in dramatic situations. Different themes can even be heard simultaneously to suggest inter-action or conflict. The musical qualities of these themes as well as the instruments used to play them help portray the essential nature of what is being represented. Thus in *Red River* the cattle theme is a simple folklike melody based mainly on the pentatonic scale, played by brass. (The pentatonic scale is found in many cowboy songs of the 'Wild West' and, since it is an ancient scale, suggests primitiveness and innocence.) The Red River theme is a grand melody played by high strings. (These two themes are given on page 17.)

In 'Red River Crossing' the music accompanies the scene in which a huge herd of more than 6000 cattle are driven across the mighty Red River. Tiomkin's score not only evokes a sense of time and place but vividly suggests the raw energy and weight of physical presence involved in making the difficult crossing.

After you have become familiar with the two themes used in 'Red River Crossing', listen to the music; then answer the questions below.

COMPOSER PROFILE

Ukrainian-born composer and concert pianist Dmitri Tiomkin (1894–1979) moved to New York in the early 1920s, and instantly became fascinated with American music. After studying and absorbing the techniques of the leading American composers of the time Tiomkin moved in 1929 to Hollywood, where he gradually made a name for himself as a composer for the new 'talking films'. His first important score was for Frank Capra's film *Lost Horizon* in 1937. This was the beginning of a long career as a film composer which lasted until 1971 and saw the creation of over 100 important film scores. He is most famous for the many scores he wrote for the classic western epics made in the 1940s and 1950s, such as *Duel in the Sun* (1946), and *Red River* (1948), as well as *High Noon* (1952), for which he made motion picture history by winning two Oscars—one for the score and one for the theme song 'Do Not Forsake Me O My Darlin' '. Tiomkin's music is in the grand, European orchestral tradition; however, it is marked with a strong affinity for the American landscape (especially the West) and its colourful characters.

 ## Listening activity

Answer these questions on 'Red River Crossing'.

1. What happens to the pitch in the introduction? What effect does this change of pitch create?
2. What theme is heard after the introduction?
3. On which scale is the theme mainly based?
4. Why does the composer use this particular scale?
5. Which instrumental families predominate in this section?
6. Why are these instruments featured? (What effect is the composer aiming to achieve?)
7. How is variation achieved in the third appearance of the theme? (Mention three ways.)
8. What solo stringed instrument plays the theme in this section? Why is this instrument used?
9. What is heard against the cattle theme at the end?

 ## Practical activity

Sing 'Do Not Forsake Me O My Darlin' ' by Dmitri Tiomkin, the award-winning song from *High Noon*, given in the *Score Book*.

THE BASIC PLOT
of *Red River*

Texan cattle baron Tom Dunson decides to drive a huge herd of cattle to be sold in the north. Along the way there are stampedes, battles with native Americans, gunfights, food shortages, desertion and a mutiny, resulting in Dunson's adopted son Matthew taking control of the drive. Dunson swears revenge. The film climaxes at Abilene, the point of destination. Dunson arrives and fires a hail of bullets at his son, who refusés to go for his gun. The two have a brutal fist fight but they make up their differences after Matthew's girlfriend intervenes with a gunshot, rebuking them for stupidly trying to kill each other.

Themes used in 'Red River Crossing'

Dmitri Tiomkin

Cattle theme

(Play 8ve lower than written.)

Red River theme

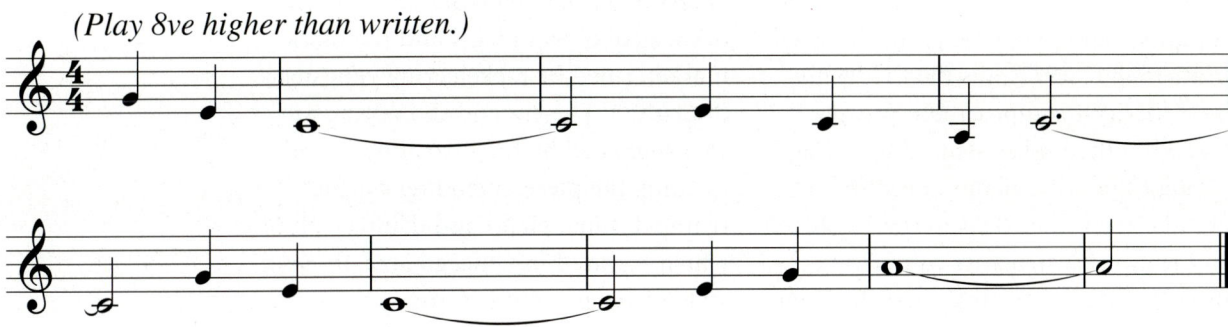

(Play 8ve higher than written.)

'THE ENTERTAINER'
from *THE STING*
(Music by SCOTT JOPLIN, arranged by MARVIN HAMLISCH)

The piano rag, 'The Entertainer', became a radio favourite and achieved worldwide popularity after being used as background music in *The Sting* (1973). A number of Scott Joplin's classic rags (see page 19), arranged by Marvin Hamlisch, were featured in the film and this sparked a renewed interest in the classically trained African-American composer and pianist. Joplin, who lived from 1868 to 1917, was the first genuine American composer and was regarded as the undisputed 'King of Rag'.

Ragtime was a piano music style popular from the 1890s to the 1930s and featured a structure comprising three or four contrasting sections often repeated, with a bright march tempo, **duple metre** (two beats in the bar), regular left-hand rhythm and a syncopated right-hand melody. (**Syncopation** is the accenting of a beat or part of a beat that is not normally accented.) The use of rags in *The Sting* evokes the atmosphere of the prohibition era in America (1920–33) when drinking more than 0.5% alcohol was illegal and the black market, ruled by racketeering gangsters, flourished. The era and the setting are also suggested by the instruments performing the piece, including clarinet, trumpet, tuba, piano and drums—all of which featured in **Chicago jazz**, the jazz style of the prohibition era.

🔺 **Con man Henry Gondorff (Paul Newman) in the fake bookie joint in The Sting**

The first 16-bar section of 'The Entertainer' is given below for you to play. When you are familiar with it, listen to the piece while following the melodic line in the *Score Book*. Hamlisch's arrangement of 'The Entertainer' omits part of Joplin's rag and is in **rondo form** (a formal structure involving at least five sections: ABACA). The arranger has provided variations of timbre within the sections by constantly changing the instrumentation. As you listen, identify the main instruments in each section.

After you have heard the music, study the score and note the various ways in which syncopation is achieved. They include the use of: (1) the rhythmic pattern ♪♩♪; (2) ties, the tied note being the note normally accented; and (3) semiquaver rests on the first beat of the bar (see bars 55, 57 and 59, and so on). Notice also the various note groupings of semiquavers and quavers to equal crotchet beats. These are given below, with their time names. You will notice that the stems in the note groupings are joined to make the value of one crotchet beat. This follows the rule that note stems should be joined according to the value of the beat.

ti - ka - ti -ka, ti - ti -ka, ti - ka -ti, syn-co -pa, tim - ka

The Entertainer

Scott Joplin

THE BASIC PLOT of *The Sting*

It is the year 1936 and two small-time con men, Johnny Hooker (Robert Redford) and Henry Gondorff (Paul Newman), tangle with a Chicago gangster, his band of thugs and a crooked policeman. Determined to avenge a friend's murder they make plans to 'sting' the gangster, Doyle Lonnegan (Robert Shaw), out of a fortune. Hooker and Gondorff set up a fake bookie joint and Lonnegan, after testing the system for traps, wagers $500 000 at 4-to-1 odds expecting to collect $2 million. However, FBI agents arrive to 'bust' the operation. Lonnegan escapes, helped by the crooked policeman, leaving his money behind. The betting parlour is dismantled and everyone gets their share of the money, including the con-man leader of the FBI agents.

Practical activity

Sing 'Ragtime Sing-Along' in the *Score Book*.

Written activity

Listen again to the A and B sections of 'The Entertainer' following the full score in the *Score Book*. Notice the way the left hand is written with a low bass note followed by a higher chord, in a 'jump bass' style, and the way the chords are written in the same pitch area of the keyboard. Given below is the right-hand part for an eight-bar rag. Write a left-hand jump bass accompaniment based on the indicated chords.

Simple duple time

The time signature for the 'The Entertainer' is $\frac{2}{4}$ —two crotchet beats in the bar. The upper figure tells us exactly how many beats there are in the bar and the lower figure tells us that the value of each beat is a crotchet or quarter note (a crotchet is one quarter of a semibreve). Because 'The Entertainer' has crotchet beats it is said to be written in **simple time,** and since there are two beats in the bar its time signature $\frac{2}{4}$ is described as **simple duple.**

Note: Music that has quaver beats or minim beats is also written in simple time; therefore $\frac{2}{8}$ is simple duple with two quaver beats in the bar and $\frac{2}{2}$ is simple duple with two minim beats in the bar.

The Sting **won seven Oscars: Best Picture, Best Director, Best Screenplay, Best Art Direction–Set Decoration, Best Editing, Best Musical Adaptation and Best Costume Design.**

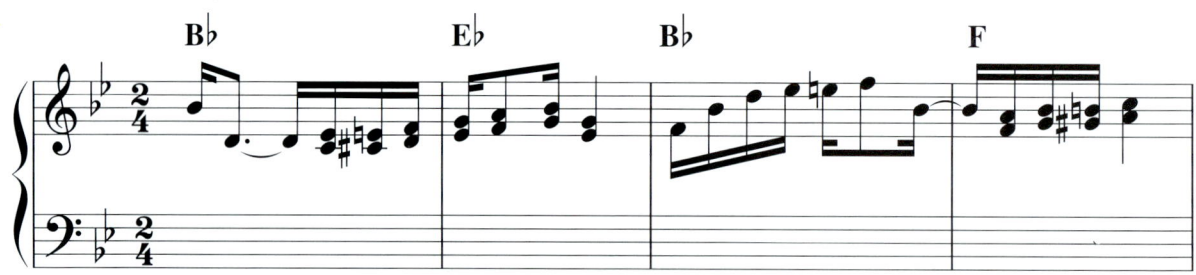

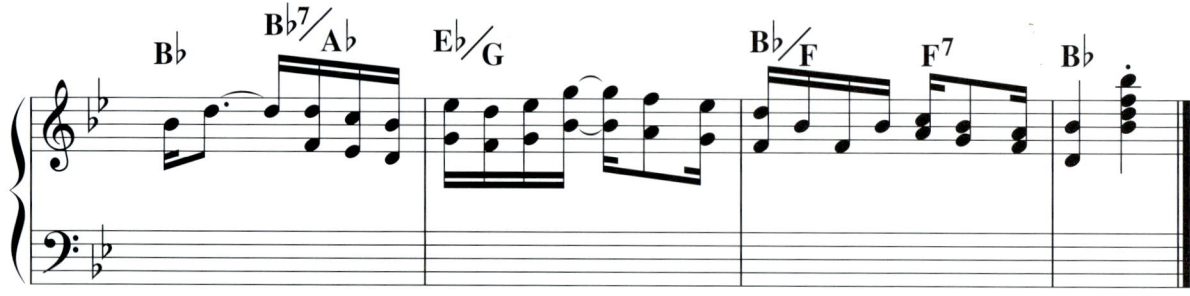

Practical activities

1. Clap the following rhythmic patterns. (Say them in time names first.)

2. Your teacher will divide the class into four groups, each group having a particular instrumental timbre, for example wooden instruments, drums, metal instruments and shakers. The four patterns above are then performed simultaneously, one group to each pattern.

 Written activities

1. Correct the mistakes in the grouping of the notes in the following music.

2. Complete the bars with the number of notes required, joining the stems according to the beats.

4 notes   6 notes   4 notes   6 notes

 Aural activity

Notate the simple duple rhythmic patterns played to you by your teacher.

'WALTZ' (RICHARD RODNEY BENNETT)

from *MURDER ON THE ORIENT EXPRESS*

The 1974 film *Murder on the Orient Express* is one of many adaptations of novels by the English author Agatha Christie (1890–1976). Featuring her famous Belgian detective Hercule Poirot (played by Albert Finney), the classic 'whodunit' murder-mystery is set in the early 1930s on the Orient Express, a luxury steam train which ran from Istanbul to Calais from 1883 to 1977 and was frequented by the international elite and the upper classes of Europe. To match the sumptuousness of the train's decor and the elegance and style of the passengers, some of whom are aristocrats and members of European

royalty, British composer Richard Rodney Bennett (born 1936) produced a rich, orchestral score which evokes the glories of Europe in the nineteenth century, a time when the aristocracy held sway. This evocative quality can be heard in the brilliant 'Waltz', used when the train pulls out of the Istanbul railway station. In **triple metre** (three beats to the bar), the music not only pictures the turning motion of the wheels in its ONE-two-three rhythm, it refers back to the Viennese waltz which was danced at the grand balls at the Emperor's court in Vienna in the second half of the nineteenth century,

⬤ *Ingrid Bergman, in the role of Greta Ohlsson, the African missionary, who was awarded an Oscar for Best Supporting Actress in* Murder on the Orient Express

the time when the Orient Express first began to run. The music's old-fashioned, nostalgic quality perfectly matches many of the characters in the film who are desperately clinging to the past. It also has a light-hearted quality which creates a sense of fun and adventure.

The main theme of 'Waltz' is used throughout the film when the train is in motion. The theme is in ternary form ABA[1]. (**Ternary form** is a formal structure involving three sections, ABA.) The A section of this rousing theme is given on page 24 for you to perform, as you will need to be familiar with it before you hear the piece.

'Waltz' begins in a very descriptive way with a long introduction that builds up slowly to the first appearance of the main theme. Listen to the piece, following the 'Listening outline'.

COMPOSER PROFILE

English composer, singer and pianist Richard Rodney Bennett (born 1936) has had international success in a variety of fields, including film and television scores, symphonies, concertos, operas, choral works, jazz pieces and educational music for children. He began writing for films in the late 1950s and his best-known scores are for *Nicholas and Alexandra* (1971), *Murder on the Orient Express* (1974), *Equus* (1977) and most recently *Four Weddings and a Funeral* (1994).

Listening outline

Introduction ♦ **Long, soft, low and dark sounds with some isolated percussion notes set a misty, late-night scene and suggest a sinister adventure is about to begin**
♦ **A four-note fragment of the main melody, followed by rapidly ascending woodwind notes suggesting rising steam, is heard in anticipation of the coming train ride (repeated three more times)**
♦ **Another fragment of the melody, this time with a fifth note added, also repeated, increases the anticipation**
♦ **A sudden loud, full orchestral fanfare, synchronised with the illumination of the train's headlamp, signals departure**

Theme .... ♦ **A gush of steam and then the A section melody, with some staccato articulation, begins *accelerando* (gradually becoming faster) on low strings, picturing the train slowly and laboriously pulling out of the station; it is repeated an octave higher**
♦ **B section melody with contrasting articulation (*legato*—smoothly, well connected) and contour (shape)**
♦ **A[1] section**

Interlude ... ♦ **A shortened form of the Introduction with the four-note fragment of the melody heard four times**

Theme .... ♦ **A section with fuller orchestration**
♦ **B section varied, played by woodwinds and glockenspiel, with cross-rhythms resulting from the melody instruments playing a pattern of two against a pattern of three in the accompaniment**
♦ **A[1] section**

THE BASIC PLOT of *Murder on the Orient Express*

The famous Belgian detective, Hercule Poirot, is travelling on the Orient Express when the train is caught in the snow. When one of the passengers is stabbed to death in his sleep, Poirot immediately begins investigating. His suspects include all of the passengers, a bizarre group among whom are an African missionary, two Hungarian royals, an English officer, a Russian aristocrat, a German lady's maid and the director of the railroad line. After much cross-examination, the brilliant Belgian detective, using his 'little grey cells', untangles the web of intrigue and solves the mystery.

Waltz

Richard Rodney Bennett

Note: The dots placed above or below some of the notes indicate that they are to be played *staccato*—short and detached.

Simple triple time

The time signature for 'Waltz' is $\frac{3}{4}$ —three crotchet beats in the bar. Because 'Waltz' has crotchet beats it is said to be written in simple time, and since there are three beats in the bar its time signature is described as **simple triple**.

Note: Other simple triple time signatures include $\frac{3}{8}$ and $\frac{3}{2}$.

Practical activities

1. In two groups perform cross-rhythms. The first group claps a two-beat pattern while the second group simultaneously claps a three-beat pattern.
2. Clap the following rhythmic patterns. (Say them in time names first.)

3. Divide again in four groups as you did for the simple duple patterns and perform the rhythmic patterns above simultaneously.

 ## Written activities

1. Correct the mistakes in the grouping of the notes in the following music.

2. Complete the bars with the number of notes required.

      3 notes   5 notes   6 notes   7 notes

 ## Aural activity

Notate the simple triple rhythmic patterns played to you by your teacher.

 ## Practical activity

Sing the waltz 'Moon River' by Henry Mancini (see page 72) from the film *Breakfast at Tiffany's*, given in the *Score Book*.

'ON OUR SELECTION' (PETER BEST)

from *DAD AND DAVE ON OUR SELECTION*

The 1995 film *Dad and Dave On Our Selection* is based on the stories of Queensland writer Steele Rudd (1868–1935). Set on the Darling Downs in the late nineteenth century, the film traces the hardships encountered by a family of pioneers who try to eke out a living on their drought-stricken plot of land, or 'selection'. The motley group of early Australian 'battlers' is led by the blustering but lovable Dad (played by Leo McKern) and Mother (Joan Sutherland) whose quiet dignity and resolve hold the family together. Despite the adversities, however, the film is not all gloom and doom. The various scenes (each based on a chapter from Rudd's book) are told with a great sense of comedy and fun as Dad and his family come up against trial after trial: snakes and spiders; the rich and villainous neighbour, J. P. Riley, who continually plots to take away Dad's land; a mad stranger who runs amok with an axe; a wayward son who 'deserts' the family to work for Riley; and so on.

As a way of setting the scene of hardship, the film begins with a song, the lyrics of which explain the terrible conditions on the Rudds' farm and the virtual hopelessness of the situation. Written by the Australian film composer Peter Best and sung by the well-known country and western singer John Williamson, the song is in **quadruple metre** (four beats in the bar) and is performed in a lazy, light-hearted manner which sets the tone of the film from the outset. The outback drawl of the singer as well as the use of guitars and accordian evoke the sound of the country bush band, so popular at dances in nineteenth century rural Australia. (A typical bush band is actually featured at a country dance in the film.) The song is unmistakably Australian—laid back, with a larrikin 'she'll be right, mate' philosophy and performed in a folk style. It is an excellent example of how music can effectively set the time and place in a film.

Listen to 'On Our Selection' while following the score in the *Score Book* and note the various ways the song evokes a sense of time and place.

▲ The poster for the 1932 film of *On Our Selection*

THE BASIC PLOT of *Dad and Dave On Our Selection*

The film does not really have a plot, but is more a series of episodes, each introduced with a title 'slide' like the chapter heading of a book. The various episodes deal with trying to tame the land and outsmart the evil Riley. There are also comic scenes involving a mad swaggie, Cranky Jack, who loses his senses each time he looks into a mirror, believing he sees his dead father come back to haunt him, and the various incompetent courting attempts of the shy young males—Dave, and Sandy Taylor who woos Kate Rudd through song. The film finishes on a triumphant note with Dad running for parliament (and winning), as he feels this is the only way to defeat the Rileys of the world and get a better deal for the battling farmer like himself.

The 1995 film *Dad and Dave On Our Selection* is the third film based on Steele Rudd's popular stories. There was a silent movie in 1920, and one by Ken G. Hall in 1932 which was enormously popular. In 1979 Sydney stage director George Whaley wrote a theatrical version which played to packed houses. It was seen by film producer Anthony Buckley who believed it was high time to reintroduce Rudd's colourful characters to a new generation of Australians. Sixteen years later his dream was realised. The new film pays homage to the old ones by starting in sepia and a square format like a silent movie.

COMPOSER PROFILE

Australian composer Peter Best (born in 1943) has written many scores for films, television and musical theatre. He has also contributed songs (both words and music) for such films as *The Adventures of Barry McKenzie* (1972), *The Picture Show Man* (1977), *Rebel* (1985), *Dad and Dave On Our Selection* (1995) and *Doing Time for Patsy Cline* (1997). Best, who composes, orchestrates and conducts his own scores, has received AFI Best Score awards for his work on *The Picture Show Man*, *Rebel* and *Dad and Dave On Our Selection*, and APRA Score awards for *Crocodile Dundee* (1986), *Crocodile Dundee II* (1988) and *Muriel's Wedding* (1994). *Dad and Dave On Our Selection* also won the Film Critic's Circle music award.

Simple quadruple time

The time signature for 'On Our Selection' is $\frac{4}{4}$—four crotchet beats in the bar. Because 'On Our Selection' has crotchet beats it is said to be written in simple time, and since there are four beats in the bar its time signature $\frac{4}{4}$ is described as **simple quadruple**.

Note: Other simple quadruple time signatures include $\frac{4}{8}$ and $\frac{4}{2}$, and C which stands for **common time** and means four crotchet beats in the bar.

 Practical activities

1. Sing 'On Our Selection' as you improvise a rhythmic accompaniment on appropriate percussion instruments.
2. Clap the following rhythmic patterns. (Say them in time names first.)

3. Divide again in four groups as you did for the simple triple patterns and perform the rhythmic patterns simultaneously.

Written activities

1. Correct the mistakes in the grouping of the notes in the following music.

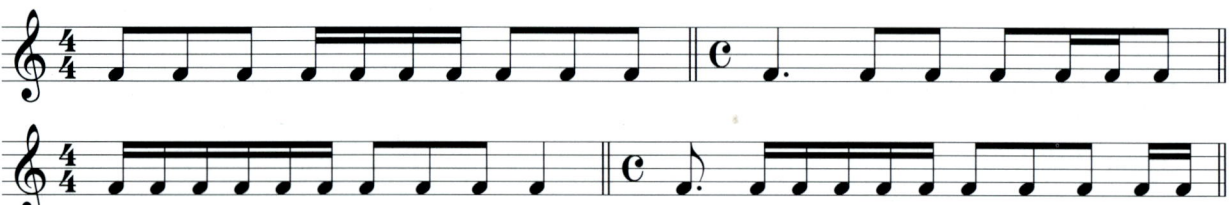

2. Complete the bars with the number of notes required.

     6 notes   6 notes   6 notes   6 notes

 Aural activity

Notate the simple quadruple rhythmic patterns played to you by your teacher.

Practical activity

Sing the Australian folk songs in the *Score Book*.

RESTS IN SIMPLE TIME

A whole bar of silence in any simple time is shown by a semibreve rest.

In $\frac{4}{4}$ time, a minim rest may be used for the first and second beats, or the third and fourth beats, but *never* for the second and third beats. (See the examples in 'The Battler's Ballad' in the *Score Book*.) A dotted minim rest is *never* used for three beats of silence.

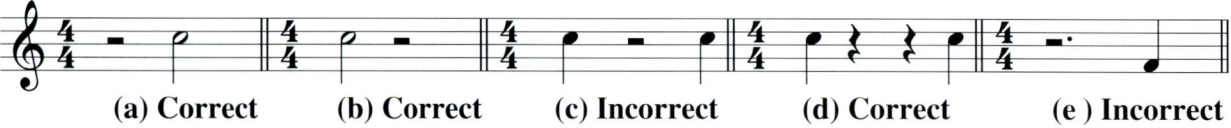

 (a) Correct **(b) Correct** **(c) Incorrect** **(d) Correct** **(e) Incorrect**

In $\frac{3}{4}$ time, always *indicate every beat* with a separate rest. *Never* use a minim rest in $\frac{3}{4}$ time. (See bars 8 and 16 of 'The Dying Stockman' in the *Score Book*.)

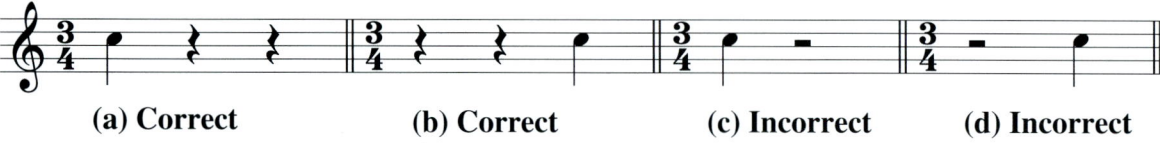

  (a) Correct   **(b) Correct**   **(c) Incorrect**   **(d) Incorrect**

Aural activities

1. Determine the time signatures of the simple time pieces played to you. Indicate these time signatures by writing $\frac{2}{4}$, $\frac{3}{4}$ or $\frac{4}{4}$.
2. Write the rhythmic patterns in $\frac{2}{4}$, $\frac{3}{4}$ or $\frac{4}{4}$ time played by your teacher.

 Written activities

1. Write these time signatures:
   (a) simple triple (b) simple duple (c) simple quadruple
2. Describe these time signatures:
   (a) $\frac{4}{4}$ (b) $\frac{2}{2}$ (c) $\frac{3}{4}$ (d) $\frac{2}{4}$ (e) **C** (f) $\frac{3}{8}$
3. Fill each of the given bars with quavers, correctly grouped according to the time signatures.

4. Complete each bar by adding rests. (Remember that you must always complete an incomplete beat first.)

SETTING WORDS TO RHYTHMS

When a composer writes a melody to a given set of words, the rhythmic pattern for the melody comes from the natural rhythm of the words. A basic skill in writing is this ability to 'set' words to a rhythmic pattern.

Let us take the opening words of the folk song 'The Broken-Down Squatter' in the *Score Book* to see how these words have been set.

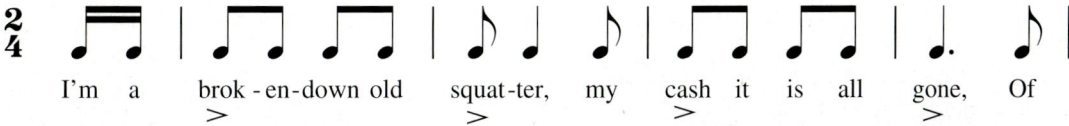

You will notice that words of more than one syllable have been divided into separate syllables using hyphens, and that there is one note given to each separate word and syllable. You will also notice that the naturally accented words or syllables occur on the strong beat of the bar, that is, on beat 1. If you say the words aloud, you will hear that the given rhythmic pattern matches the natural rhythm of the words.

The process of setting words to rhythmic patterns is summarised in the following guidelines (see page 30).

29

Guidelines for setting words to rhythmic patterns

1. Write the words, using hyphens to divide words of more than one syllable.
2. Place accent signs under the words or syllables that are accented when they are spoken.
3. Place bar lines in front of the correct accented word or syllable according to the time signature. In $\frac{2}{4}$ and $\frac{3}{4}$ time there will be one accent per bar; in $\frac{4}{4}$ time there will be two accents per bar.
   Note: If there is no accent on the first word or syllable, as in 'The Broken-Down Squatter', there will be an anacrusis of one or more notes.
4. Write rhythmic patterns that suit the way the words are spoken. The notes should be written neatly above the words.

 ## Written activities

1. Following the guidelines, set the words below to two-bar rhythmic patterns according to the given time signatures:

   $\frac{2}{4}$ Star Wars, The Sting

   $\frac{3}{4}$ Murder on the Orient Express

   $\frac{4}{4}$ Raiders of the Lost Ark, The Empire Strikes Back

   $\frac{2}{4}$ The Man from Snowy River

   $\frac{3}{4}$ The Piano, Schindler's List

   $\frac{4}{4}$ The Lion King, Batman, On Our Selection

2. Set the following couplets to rhythmic patterns of the required length in the given metres.

(a) Duple metre, eight bars long:
   The Lion King's first song is 'Circle of Life',
   With music by Elton John and lyrics by Tim Rice.

(b) Triple metre, eight bars long:
   John Williams wrote music for *Jaws* and *Jurassic Park*,
   Sabrina, E.T. and *Raiders of the Lost Ark*.

(c) Quadruple metre, four bars long:
   The theme from *Batman* was written by Danny Elfman,
   While the musical score of *Emma* is by Rachel Portman.

'TURKISH MARCH' (JEAN-BAPTISTE LULLY)

from *TOUS LES MATINS DU MONDE*

Based on a true story, the 1991 French film *Tous les Matins du Monde* is a detailed portrait of two masterful musicians in France at the end of the seventeenth century. It tells the story of the violist Monsieur de Sainte-Colombe—who after the death of his wife is left, inconsolable, to bring up his two daughters alone—and of his pupil, Marin Marais, who falls in love with Sainte-Colombe's elder daughter Madeleine but subsequently leaves her to pursue his musical ambitions as a performer, conductor and composer at the court of Louis XIV in Paris. Life of the period is faithfully portrayed as is the brilliance and grandeur of the court.

The film is set in the period of history known as the baroque period (1600–1750), the term 'baroque' referring to the highly decorated artistic style of the time. This is particularly evident in the scenes of the French court with the gilding and ornamentation of walls, ceilings and doors and the elaborate wigs and clothing of the musicians.

Much of the music in *Tous les Matins du Monde* was composed for bass viol (see page 33), one of the most important stringed instruments of the time, and therefore its use in the film helps evoke the late seventeenth century. Other baroque instruments are also featured to give a sense of time and place. For example, in the scene in the Versailles palace of King Louis XIV (pictured) a baroque orchestra performs the 'Turkish March' from the musical play *Le Bourgeois Gentilhomme*

by the Italian-born composer Jean-Baptiste Lully. Marais is seen conducting with a long tasselled stick. Orchestras of the time comprised whatever instruments were available. The 'Turkish March' features violins, bass viols, a theorbo (a type of bass lute), pipes or flutes and a military-type side drum that had evolved in Switzerland in the fifteenth century. The music is a slow, stately march in duple metre with the time signature ¢ (called **cut common time** today, meaning two minim beats to the bar). It is in a typical baroque binary dance form of two repeated sections. (**Binary form** is a formal structure involving two sections, AB.) In the performance the quavers are played as they would have been at the time, with a dotted rhythm ♩. ♪ rather than ♪ ♪, and ornamentation of trills added to the melody line in seventeenth century style. (A **trill** is a rapid alternation of a note with the note above it.)

Play the melody of the 'Turkish March' on page 32 which has been rewritten at a lower pitch for ease of playing. Then listen to the music, following the score in the *Score Book* and noting the timbres of the baroque instruments and the performing style.

▲ *The palace of Versailles*

THE BASIC PLOT
of *Tous les Matins du Monde*

The elderly musician Marin Marais (Gerard Depardieu) is remembering his past. As a youthful viol player he had gone to ask for lessons from former court musician Monsieur de Sainte-Colombe (Jean-Pierre Marielle). On the death of his wife, the grief-stricken Sainte-Colombe had forsaken the world to devote his life to his music and two young daughters. The young Marais studies with Sainte-Colombe but is banished from the house when he falls in love with Madeleine, the elder daughter (Anne Brochet). However, he continues to learn the master's craft from Madeleine. He also hides beneath the rehearsal shed and listens to Sainte-Colombe's playing. Finally, abandoning Madeleine for the glories of Louis XIV's court, Marais becomes famous as a performer, composer and conductor. Now all he has left are his memories.

COMPOSER PROFILE

The baroque composer Jean-Baptiste Lully (born in Florence in 1632, died in Paris in 1687) is credited with being the creator of French opera. He became Louis XIV's composer of dance music at the age of 21 and soon was famous as a violinist, conductor and composer. Lully composed ballets, such as *Alcidiane* (1658), for the court, dancing alongside the King in many of them. In collaboration with the French playwright Molière, he composed a series of comedy ballets including *Les Fâcheux* (The Bores, 1661), *Le Mariage Forcé* (1665), and *Le Bourgeois Gentilhomme* (1670). Lully's serious operas, which he called *'tragédies-lyriques'*, include *Persée* (1682), *Amadis de Gaule* (1684) and *Acis et Galatée* (1686). They are notable for their elaborate dance spectacles and massive choruses. Lully died from an abscess caused by striking his foot with his long baton while conducting, a baton that must have been similar to the one used by Marais in the film.

Turkish March

Jean-Baptiste Lully

Written activities

1. Write a piano reduction of the score of the 'Turkish March'.
2. Arrange the score for the instruments available in your class.

Winner of seven Césars, France's equivalent to the Oscar, including Best Film and Best Director. The soundtrack album is an all-time French best-seller.

 *Musicians at the Norwich Festival playing theorbos. A type of bass lute, the theorbo was frequently used as an accompanying instrument in baroque instrumental ensembles. It is featured in Lully's 'Turkish March' in Tous les Martins du Monde. Another instrument featured in the piece is the bass viol, a member of the viol family. The viol had a flat back, thinner strings, sloping shoulders, deeper ribs, frets, C-shaped sound holes, a flatter bridge and usually six strings. The tone was softer and thinner than that of the violin which gradually superseded the viol. Unlike violins, viols were always held downwards, the smaller ones resting between the knees and the larger ones between the legs.*

THE SIX HISTORICAL PERIODS OF MUSIC, ART AND LITERATURE

1. The medieval period .... 450 –1450
2. The renaissance period .... 1450 –1600
3. The baroque period .... 1600 –1750
4. The classical period .... 1750 –1825
5. The romantic period .... 1825 –1900
6. The twentieth century .... 1900 onwards

In any discussion about the arts the six basic periods given above serve as a general time frame. In the works of music, art and literature of each period certain elements create a characteristic style. With regard to the development of music, the first two periods are seen as 'preparatory' stages: it was during these periods that a system of musical notation evolved, forerunners of our modern instruments were invented and musical concepts such as metre, key and chord progression began to be developed. In this book at least one piece from each of the last four periods is studied.

🎼 FILM MUSIC FOR AURAL ANALYSIS

Listen to the title song from *The Picture Show Man* and 'Lara's Theme' from *Doctor Zhivago*, two pieces of film music that evoke a time and place. The first is by the Australian composer Peter Best (see page 27) and the second by the Frenchman Maurice Jarre, one of the leading film composers since the 1960s, whose scores include *Lawrence of Arabia* (1962), *Mad Max Beyond Thunderdome* (1985) and *Ghost* (1990). For each piece identify how the composer evokes the particular historical and national setting through such elements as musical style, instrumental timbre and rhythm. A brief background is given for each film so that you will understand the context of the music.

'Main Theme' (Peter Best)
from *The Picture Show Man*

The 1977 film *The Picture Show Man* tells the story of a showman in Australia in the 1920s who travels to small towns throughout the country with his moving picture show. As this is the era of silent movies such travelling shows were accompanied by music played on piano, or whatever instrument was available. Starring John Meillon, the film is filled with the atmosphere of the time.

'Lara's Theme' (Maurice Jarre)
from *Doctor Zhivago*

Doctor Zhivago (1965), winner of five Academy Awards, including one for music, is set in Russia in the early decades of the twentieth century and tells the dramatic story of the poet and doctor Zhivago before, during and after the 1917 Bolshevik revolution. The film traces his life, his marriage to an aristocrat and his ill-fated love affair with the beautiful nurse Lara against the total disruption caused by the social upheavals resulting from World War I and the communist revolution.

Activities for senior students

Composition

Write a short piece of music that would be appropriate for the main title of a film set in a particular country, for example Japan, Bolivia, Ireland or (outback) Australia. You will need to investigate the characteristics of the music of your chosen country and incorporate these into your composition. Select suitable instruments, either authentic or synthesised, that would evoke a sense of place.

Arranging

Imagine you are to provide music for a film scene set in a particular decade of the twentieth century. To evoke a sense of the time, select a piece of popular music, the style of which is characteristic of that era, and arrange it for appropriate instruments.

Create a soundtrack

Select an appropriate piece of recorded music to accompany a scene set in an identifiable time and/or place. Dub the music onto the filmed scene.

Research activity

Select three films in which the music conjures up an historical setting, for example *Braveheart*, *Little Buddha* or *The Madness of King George*. Discuss the characteristics of the music, the instruments used, the musical style and any other features that help contribute to the sense of period. If possible, notate the musical themes and provide illustrations of instruments.

Oral presentation

Using video excerpts, provide an interpretation and analysis of the music of a film that evokes a time and/or place, for example, *Forrest Gump*. You will need to discuss the characteristics of the various musical excerpts and then relate them to the particular historical period or identifiable country or location.

WORDS TO KNOW

pitch	ostinato	simple time	cut common time
volume	polyrhythms	simple duple	binary form
duration	pentatonic scale	triple metre	trill
timbre	scale	ternary form	medieval period
score	spiritual	contour	renaissance period
tempo	ragtime	cross-rhythms	baroque period
texture	duple metre	simple triple	classical period
theme	syncopation	quadruple metre	romantic period
call-and-	Chicago jazz	simple quadruple	
response	rondo form	common time	

▶ *Tom Hanks in a scene from Forrest Gump (1994). Composer Alan Silvestri portrays his happy childlike innocence through the use of a simple, high-pitched and lilting melody*

CONVEYING CHARACTER OR IDEAS

In a novel, an author can easily build up a picture of a character for the reader through words. In a film it is not so easy. The viewer cannot expect to fully understand what a character is like by simply seeing him or her on the screen. This is often where the composer comes in, being required to write music that will give clues as to the true nature of the various players. Composing for film involves cleverly manipulating such elements of music as melody, rhythm and instrumentation to give a character-study in sound. An appropriate musical style can also be used for the purposes of conveying character. Similarly, a composer can use music to convey the innermost thoughts or ideas of one or more characters. Let us investigate a few very famous examples.

'THE JAMES BOND THEME'

from *DR NO*   (Composed by MONTY NORMAN, arranged by JOHN BARRY)

In 1962 *Dr No* burst onto movie screens, introducing a new kind of exciting and sophisticated spy thriller and a cool hero, James Bond, undercover Agent 007 of Her Majesty's Secret Service, who was unlike any hero the public had seen before. Played by Sean Connery, Bond was suave, witty, cynical, fearless, daring, dangerous (he was licensed to kill), and oozed sex appeal.

Dr No also introduced many of the characters and elements that were to feature in all future Bond movies, including Bond's frustrated boss M, his secretary the flirtatious Miss Moneypenny, 'The James Bond Theme'— one of the most famous of all movie themes—and the dramatic opening sequence in which the camera follows Bond as if looking down the barrel of a gun. *Dr No* had other elements of the Bond-movie formula as well: a ruthless villain who belonged to S.P.E.C.T.R.E.— an evil organisation scheming to take over the world—beautiful girls, spectacular action sequences, chases and stunts, expensive cars, exotic locales and lavish sets and costumes.

Although the music for *Dr No* was composed by Monty Norman, the famous theme was actually arranged by the English composer John Barry, who is one of the leading film composers of the past three decades. 'The James Bond Theme' is a brilliant piece of music which cleverly conveys many of the aspects of Bond's character mentioned earlier. It begins with a loud dramatic introduction after which the volume

drops and a **melodic ostinato** (a short repeated melodic idea) is heard, suggesting mystery and lurking danger through the gradual rising and falling pitch patterns and the use of soft string instrumentation. The regular minim rhythms seem to imply the 'calm before

▲ *Sean Connery as the super-cool undercover agent James Bond 007*

the storm'. The two-bar ostinato is actually built on notes that move in small steps or **intervals** called **semitones** (see page 38), the use of which contributes strongly to the 'undercover' feeling of the music.

In the next section of the theme a melody is heard over the repeated melodic ostinato played by solo electric guitar, the hard-edged sound of which has a machine-gun-like quality. The melody features syncopation through the use of ties between the second and third beats of the bar, which contributes to the feeling of unrest. This melody also features notes moving in steps, some of which are **tones** (a tone being the interval of two semitones together), and rises repetitively up and down, not really getting anywhere. (Could this be the hero lying in wait?) Towards the end, however, the melody makes a sudden and surprising leap, upsetting its smooth contour or shape (perhaps suggesting the hero pouncing on his victim).

The third section is a complete contrast. It is loud and brassy, in a big-band, **swing** style accompanied at times by gun-like rhythms on drums. This is exciting, sophisticated music, embodying all of the flamboyant and larger-than-life characteristics that have made James Bond such a popular movie character. The melody features frequent use of semitone intervals and is highly syncopated.

After the third section the melodic ostinato is heard again, followed by the guitar melody. The piece ends with a final repetition of the ostinato and a short coda.

Learn to play 'The James Bond Theme' in the *Score Book* and then listen to the music, noting how the intervals and rhythms of the melody as well as the use of instruments help convey Bond's character.

THE BASIC PLOT of *Dr No*

In his explosive debut, film history's immortal action hero 007 (Sean Connery) is sent to Jamaica, where mysterious energy waves are interfering with US missile launches. As he uncovers the astonishing truth, 007 fights deadly assassins, and battles sexy femme fatales and even a poisonous tarantula. Together with CIA agent Felix Leiter (Jack Lord) and the beautiful Honey Ryder (Ursula Andress) 007 searches for the secret headquarters of Dr No (Joseph Wiseman), a fanatical scientist who is implementing an evil plan of world domination. (Dr No is a scary and ruthless villain, whose steel hands are capable of crushing a small bronze statue.) Only Bond with his wit, charm and skill can save the human race from a horrible fate.

COMPOSER PROFILE

John Barry was born in York, England, in 1933 and began his early career in jazz and popular music, composing original songs and producing and arranging for other British artists. In 1958 he began his successful career in film score writing which to date has seen the composition of nearly 100 scores. He has won five Oscars, including four Best Original Score awards for *Dances with Wolves* (1990), *Out of Africa* (1985), *The Lion in Winter* (1968) and *Born Free* (1966), and a Best Song award for *Born Free*. Of the many composers who have contributed scores for the 17 Bond films, Barry (who has the unique distinction of having Bond's initials) is the most prolific, having written 13. He has also written many successful popular songs, some of which are featured in his Bond films. (For example, 'From Russia With Love', 'Goldfinger', 'Diamonds are Forever' and 'Moonraker'.) He is currently ranked as one of the most talented and sought-after film composers in the world.

 ## Practical activities

1. **Sing 'Goldfinger' by John Barry, given in the *Score Book*. It is the title song from the 1964 James Bond film and incorporates the two-bar melodic ostinato from 'The James Bond Theme'.**
2. **Improvise melodies in a jazz style above the following ostinato or one of your own devising.**

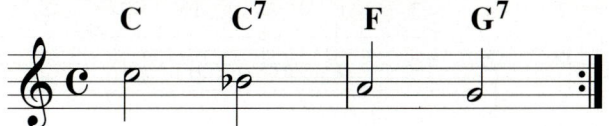

TONES AND SEMITONES

A semitone is the smallest distance or interval between two adjacent notes on the keyboard. A tone is made up of two semitones together. For example, the notes in the opening melodic ostinato of 'The James Bond Theme' move in semi-tone steps, while the steps in bar 5 (E to F♯) are tones.

On the keyboard certain white notes are a semitone apart, while others are a tone apart because they have a black note in between. Look at the diagram of the keyboard below and work out the letter names for the pairs of white notes a semitone apart and a tone apart. (The white note on the left of the diagram is C.)

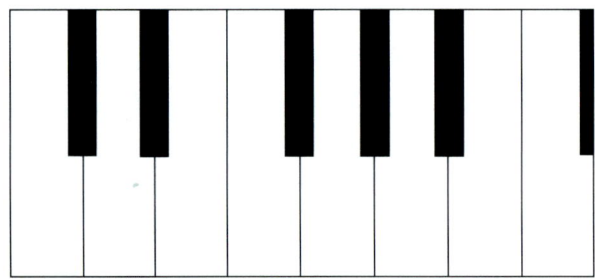

The black note to the right of a white note is called a **sharp** and is a semitone higher in pitch. It is indicated by the sign ♯ The black note to the left of a white note is called a **flat** and is a semitone lower in pitch. It is indicated by the sign ♭. Name the black notes on the keyboard above as sharps and flats.

To return a black note to its original white note pitch a **natural** sign ♮ is used, as in bar 2 of 'The James Bond Theme'. Therefore, when a natural sign cancels a sharp (as in bar 2) the pitch of the note is lowered one semitone. When a natural sign cancels a flat the pitch of the note is raised one semitone.

Given below are the white and black notes of the keyboard written as scales ascending and descending in semitone steps. In the first scale the black notes are written as sharps; in the second they are written as flats. These are **chromatic scales** because they move by semitone steps. Play them and listen to the sound.

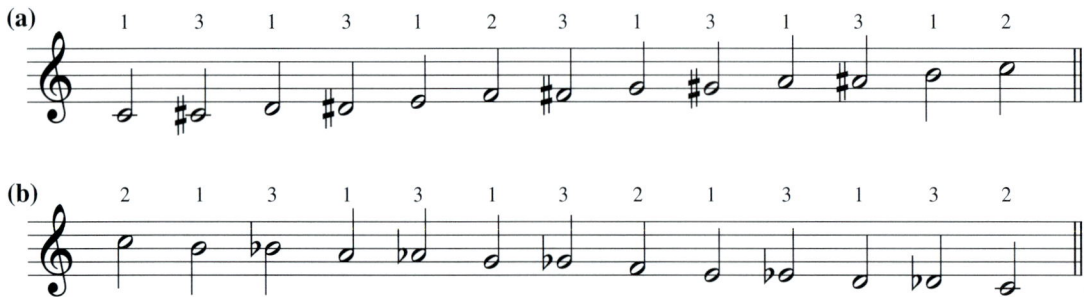

A different type of scale that moves by steps of a tone is
called a **whole-tone scale.** Play the two whole-tone scales given
below and listen to the sound. Composers sometimes use
chromatic and whole-tone scales in their music to create
special effects.

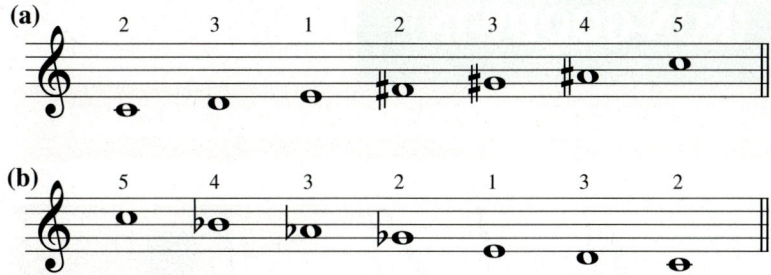

 Aural activities

1. Identify the intervals played to you as either tones or
   semitones. Also state whether the second note is higher or
   lower than the first.
2. Identify the scales played to you as either pentatonic,
   chromatic or whole-tone.

 Written activities

1. By referring to the keyboard, work out which notes are a
   semitone away from the given notes (either up or down as
   required) and write them after the given notes.

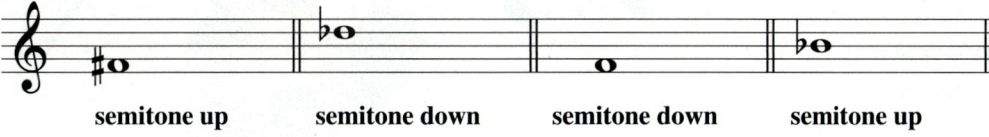

2. By looking at the keyboard, work out which notes are a
   tone away from the given notes (either up or down as
   required) and write them after the given notes.

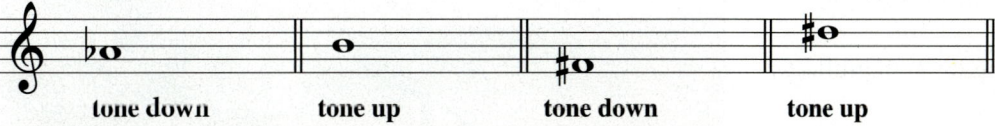

3. By using a sharp, flat or natural sign against the second of
   each pair of notes, raise or lower the first note a semitone
   as directed.

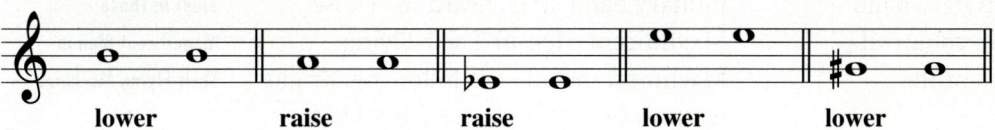

'THOSE MAGNIFICENT MEN IN THEIR FLYING MACHINES' (RON GOODWIN)

from *THOSE MAGNIFICENT MEN IN THEIR FLYING MACHINES*

'Those Magnificent Men in Their Flying Machines' by the English composer Ron Goodwin is the theme song from the 1965 film of the same name. It is heard with the credits at the beginning of the film which concerns a great airplane race held in about 1910 and involving international conflicts, cheating and romance. It serves to portray the character of the intrepid pilots who are daring, foolhardy, comical and happy-go-lucky as they provide their spectacular show.

The portrayal of character in the song comes about largely as a result of the **military band style** of the music. These bands, made up of different types of woodwind, brass and percussion instruments, were very popular in Europe in the early 1900s, the time in which the film is set. They were—and still are—to be seen and heard at entertaining spectacles held out of doors and involving large numbers of people. Thus several aspects of the airmen's character are conveyed through the military band style:

- they love putting on a magnificent display;
- they love entertaining large crowds;
- they love the outdoors.

The sound of a military band is loud, brash, lively and colourful—further characteristics of the magnificent men.

▲ *A daring mid-air stunt in* **Those Magnificent Men in Their Flying Machines**

Musical characteristics of the military band style, heard in 'Those Magnificent Men in Their Flying Machines', include the following: bright tempos; two-beat metres (suitable for marching); two-beat, oom-pah bass lines played by tuba; lively rhythms involving **triplets** (three notes played in the time of two of the same value), for example 'up tiddlee up up'; syncopation; and melodies involving many repeated notes.

The melody of the song is also marked by the use of octave leaps which picture the somersaulting movement of the airmen's planes. In bars 9–10 of the score a high note is used for 'up' and a low note, one octave lower, is used for 'down'. This is a clever example of **word painting**, whereby a musical element (in this case pitch) is used to picture the meaning of the lyrics. Note that in the soundtrack recording of the song, a swanee whistle, a novelty instrument that produces a whistling note that slides up and down, is used to reinforce the word painting and add amusing aural effects. (Trombone slides are also used for humorous effects.) These devices bring out another aspect of the airmen's character—their comical side.

'Those Magnificent Men in Their Flying Machines' is in ternary form and can be represented by the letters AA'BA as follows:

A — bars 1–24 sung by men's chorus
A' — repeat of bars 1–24 played by full band without lyrics
B — bars 24–40 men's chorus with banjo added to the accompaniment for a bright sound
A — the same as the opening

The melody of 'Those Magnificent Men in Their Flying Machines', together with the 'oom-pah' bass line written in the bass staff (see page 44), is given in the *Score Book*. Learn to sing the song then listen to the soundtrack recording of it as you view the opening credits of the film.

THE MAJOR SCALE

If the melody notes of different pitch of the first eight bars of 'Those Magnificent Men in Their Flying Machines' were written out with ascending letter names, they would appear as the scale written below.

This scale has the pattern of intervals T T S T T T S, where T indicates a tone and S indicates a semitone. This is the pattern of the **major scale**, and it is the use of this scale that gives the song its appropriate happy, bright sound. Because C is the first note of the major scale written above, it is called the C major scale.

The major scale may be sung to solfa syllables as given below.

doh   re   mi   fa   soh   la   ti   doh

If we were to write a number under the solfa names to indicate the particular note of the scale referred to by these solfa names, the numbers would represent the **scale degrees**, that is, the position of each note in the scale counting upwards from the lowest note. Study the example given below, which shows the scale degrees.

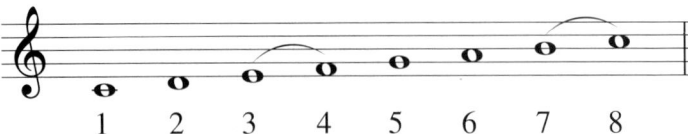

Because 'Those Magnificent Men in Their Flying Machines' is based on the scale of C major it is said to be written in the key of C major (The **key** is the name of the scale on which a piece of music is based.) You will notice that the music also contains some added sharps. Sharps, flats and naturals placed in front of notes are called **accidentals**.

If we applied the T T S T T T S pattern to a series of eight notes written ascending in alphabetical order starting on G we would form the G major scale given below.

Any piece of music based on the notes of this scale would therefore be written in the key of G major. If the song 'Those Magnificent Men in Their Flying Machines' was in the key of G major, the melody of the first eight bars would appear as it is below.

Because the melody uses the G major scale all Fs need a sharp sign in front of them. (In bar 6 the sharp at the beginning of the bar means that all Fs in that bar are actually F sharps.) To avoid having to continually use accidentals the music is written as follows.

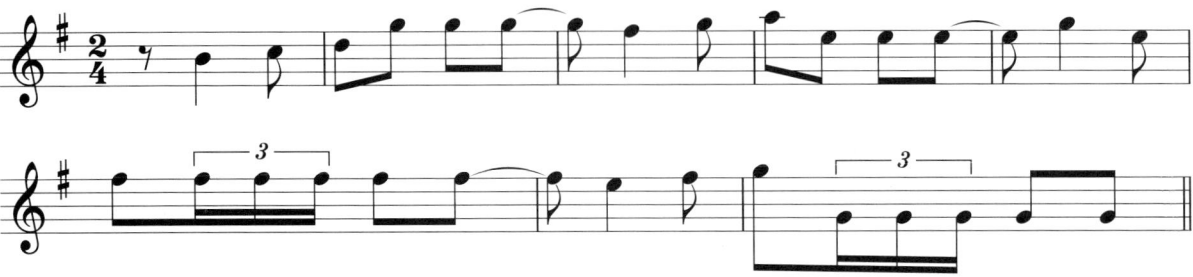

The sign written after the clef is the **key signature** of G major. It means that every F in the piece must be played as F sharp.

When the T T S T T T S pattern is applied to a scale of eight notes starting on F we form the F major scale, and music based on this scale is written in the key of F major.

In F major all Bs must be played as B flat. The first eight bars of 'Those Magnificent Men in Their Flying Machines' in F major would be written with a key signature as follows.

It is possible to form a major scale on any note of the keyboard by applying the T T S T T T S pattern. This will result in 12 different major scales. The key signatures for these are given on page 144. Notice that the order of sharps and flats is always the same. A piece of music written in C major does not need a key signature, as the C major scale does not contain any sharps or flats.

 Written activities

1. Write the scales of G, D, F and B flat major one octave ascending using minims. Do not use a key signature, but write accidentals in front of notes that require them. Mark semitones with slurs.

2. Write the scales of G, D, F and B flat major one octave descending using crotchets. Write a key signature for each scale and mark the semitones with slurs.

3. Identify the major keys that have the following key signatures.

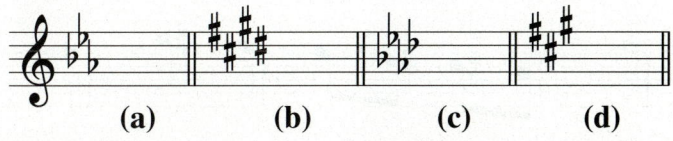

 Aural activities

1. A number of different scales will be played to you. Identify the major scales.

2. Identify the particular scales played to you as pentatonic, chromatic, whole-tone or major.

3. Notate two-bar major melodies played to you by your teacher.

THE BASS STAFF

You will notice that two staves with different clefs are used for the arrangement in the *Score Book* of the song 'Those Magnificent Men in Their Flying Machines'. The first is the treble clef and the second is the bass clef. The treble clef is used mainly for notes written above middle C while the bass clef is used mainly for notes written below middle C.

Study the diagram to the right to understand the letter names of the notes on the bass staff.

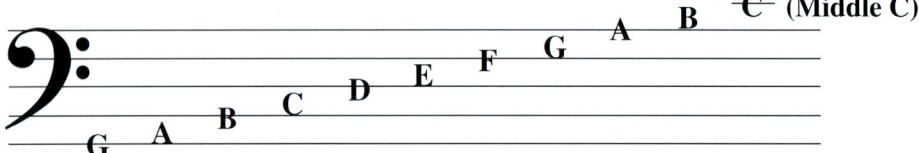

Note the position of middle C when it is used with a bass clef and compare it with middle C in bars 7 and 10 of the song melody used with a treble clef.

The lines and spaces of the bass staff may be remembered by saying the following:

- *Lines:* Great Birds Do Fly Away
- *Spaces:* All Cows Eat Grass

Note: In the song arrangement the bass staff music has been written an octave higher than the bass is playing to make it easier to read.

Before you do the following 'Written activities', practise drawing some bass clefs, using the clef above as a guide.

 ## Written activities

1. Write the letter names of the notes on the bass staff of bars 2–9 of 'Those Magnificent Men in Their Flying Machines'.
2. Write semibreves on the bass staff to spell the following words. If a word has two letters that are the same, write the second letter in a position different from the first. Write the letters underneath the notes.
   (a) FADED (b) BADGE (c) CAGED (d) BAGGED (e) CABBAGE
3. Write the scales of C, G, D, F and B flat major ascending on the bass staff in crotchets. Use key signatures where they are required and mark the semitones with slurs.

4. Write the scales of C, G, D, F and B flat major descending on the bass staff in minims. Do not use key signatures. Mark the semitones with slurs.
5. Work out the key of each of the following melodies by studying the accidentals used in them.

Practical activities

1. Learn to play the scales of C, G, D, F and B flat major ascending and descending.

2. Learn to play the scales of A, E, E flat and A flat major ascending and descending.

A MOVIE THEME TO PLAY

The 1966 film *Born Free*, about the lioness Elsa who was raised by two game wardens in Kenya, won Oscars for Best Original Score and Title Song. John Barry's famous melody, which is given below, features many triplets—three notes played in the time of two of the same value. Triplets are indicated by a slur or bracket (as here) and the figure 3.

Born Free   John Barry

'THE HEART ASKS PLEASURE FIRST'

from *THE PIANO*   (MICHAEL NYMAN)

The Piano was one of the most unusual films of 1994. Directed by New Zealander Jane Campion, it tells the story of the mute Ada, who leaves Scotland in the middle of the nineteenth century to marry an unknown man, Stewart, living in rugged country in New Zealand's South Island. Ada is shown in the film making a spectacular arrival in her new homeland in a Maori boat which also transports her most prized possession—her piano. It is the piano that gives her consolation in her uncertain situation and which enables her to express her innermost feelings. Unfortunately her new husband Stewart does not understand her need for the piano and it is left on the beach, a stark and powerful symbol of civilisation in an uncivilised land.

'The Heart Asks Pleasure First' is first played by Ada on her beloved piano, still in its packing case on the beach, after she has persuaded her new neighbour George Baines to take her back to it. The rippling music, with its simple hypnotic melody and constant semiquaver accompaniment, portrays her as a naive, tender romantic, restless and full of longing for happiness. It is as if she is under the piano's spell and it is only when she is playing that she is truly happy. The melody uses the notes of the **A natural minor scale**, that is, the white notes of the piano from A to A or la to la¹ (see below). This scale, also

THE BASIC PLOT of *The Piano*

In the middle of the nineteenth century, Ada (Holly Hunter) and her daughter Flora (Anna Paquin) leave Scotland for New Zealand after Ada's arranged marriage to Stewart (Sam Neill), who lives in the rugged country of the South Island. Ada, a mute, is unable to communicate properly with her new husband, and her most valued possession, a piano, is at first left on a deserted beach because Stewart cannot understand Ada's need for it. When Stewart sells the piano to their neighbour George Baines (Harvey Keitel), Ada is devastated. She arranges to earn the piano back by giving George piano lessons—but he insists that there be certain conditions attached as well. Reluctantly she agrees and slowly their relationship turns to love. Stewart becomes insanely jealous and attacks Ada. She flees by boat with Flora, Baines and the piano.

The Piano was nominated for eight Academy Awards, including Best Picture, and was the winner of the awards for Best Actress, Best Supporting Actress and Best Original Screenplay.

called the **Aeolian mode**, has the sad quality so often associated with folk song, and reflects Ada's sadness at her circumstances.

Learn to play the excerpt of main melody of 'The Heart Asks Pleasure First' given on the following page and then listen to the recording following the music in the *Score Book*.

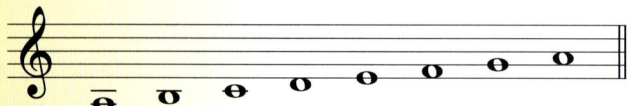

A natural minor scale or Aeolian mode

'It was a real challenge to write this music, because it is absolutely crucial to the film. If you delve into the reasons for the piano's existence, you realise that the establishing of a musical language is crucial. Since Ada doesn't speak, the piano music doesn't simply have the usual expressive role but becomes a substitute for her voice. The sound of the piano becomes her character, her mood, her expressions, her unspoken dialogue. It has to convey the messages she is putting across about her feelings towards Baines, during the piano lessons, and these differ from lesson to lesson as the relationship develops. I've had to create a kind of aural scenography which is as important as the locations, as important as the costumes.'

MICHAEL NYMAN

COMPOSER PROFILE

Michael Nyman, music critic, author and composer, was born in London in 1944. He has composed vocal and choral works, music for orchestra, chamber groups, operas, ballet, dance, television and 19 film soundtracks, including *The Piano* in 1994. He has also written for the Michael Nyman Band. An interest in folk music led him to collect folk songs in Romania, and this interest in folk music is evident in his use of simple Scottish popular and folk songs as a basis for Ada's piano pieces.

The Heart Asks Pleasure First

Michael Nyman

Note: The theme above is written in compound time (see page 48) in which the beats are dotted crotchets.

THE PIANO SCORE

Study the score of 'The Heart Asks Pleasure First', which was written specifically for the piano. You will notice that two staves are used for piano music, and these are joined on the left by a staff line and a brace. (Compare the square bracket of earlier scores.) A treble clef is used for the upper staff mainly for notes above middle C played by the right hand. A bass clef is used for the lower staff mainly for notes below middle C played by the left hand. In this score, after bar 10, you will notice that a bass clef is placed on the upper staff. This indicates that in the following bars the right hand will be playing notes below middle C. The bass clef is used here instead of the treble clef in order to avoid a large number of ledger lines. Near the end of bar 12 the right hand once again returns to the treble clef. The composer's directions for performance are placed at the beginning of the music. The Italian words *sempre cantabile ma marcato il melodia* mean 'always in a singing style with the melody marked or accented'.

COMPOUND TIME

'The Heart Asks Pleasure First' commences with a $\frac{12}{8}$ time signature, changes to $\frac{9}{8}$ in bar 5, $\frac{6}{8}$ in bar 6 and back to $\frac{12}{8}$ in bar 7. If you study the left-hand part of bar 1 in the score you will notice that each group of six semiquavers is placed above a dotted crotchet. There are four groups in the bar; therefore this indicates that there are four dotted crotchet beats in the bar. In bar 5 there are three groups of six semiquavers with three dotted crotchet beats, and in bar 6 there are two groups making two dotted crotchet beats. Music that has dotted beats such as $\frac{6}{8}$ is said to be written in **compound time**, whereas music that has minim or crotchet beats is in simple time. Beats in compound time always divide into three subdivisions or pulses. Study the diagram (figure A, top right) which shows the subdivisions of compound time beats. Note that the quaver and semiquaver stems are always joined according to the beats.

Other frequently used subdivisions in compound time include those in the figure B, above right (which are found in the Scottish folk songs in the *Score Book*).

The upper figure of a compound time signature shows the number of pulses in a bar. The lower figure shows the value of each pulse. To find the number of beats in a bar of compound time, divide the upper figure by three. To find the value of each beat, add the value of three pulses together. Therefore $\frac{6}{8}$ is

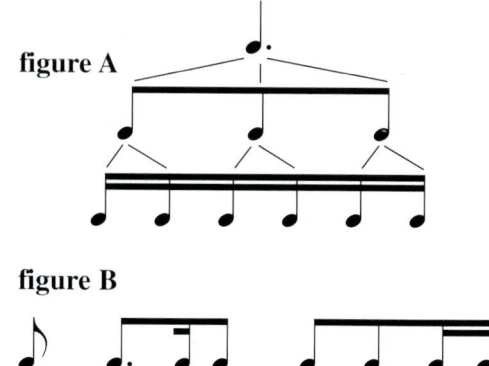

figure A

figure B

described as **compound duple** (two ♩. beats to the bar), $\frac{9}{8}$ is **compound triple** (three ♩. beats to the bar) and $\frac{12}{8}$ is **compound quadruple** (four ♩. beats to the bar).

Note that in bars 9 and 10 of 'The Heart Asks Pleasure First' the normal ♩. subdivision of the right-hand melody is altered to ♩ ♩ dividing the dotted crotchet beat into two equal parts while the left-hand part retains the normal ♩ ♪ subdivisions. This produces cross-rhythms and creates an unsettling effect that reflects Ada's mood.

 Practical activities

1. Clap the compound time patterns given below. (Say them in time names first.)

2. **Divide in four groups as you did for the simple time patterns and perform the rhythmic patterns above simultaneously.**

3. Sing the Scottish folk songs in the *Score Book*. 'I'll Bid My Heart Be Still' uses the notes of the A natural minor scale; 'Ye Banks and Braes o' Bonnie Doon' is in compound duple time and uses the notes of the G pentatonic scale; and 'Rothesay-O' is in compound quadruple time and uses the notes of the **Mixolydian mode**, which has another arrangement of tones and semitones.

4. Working in pairs, improvise melodies based on the Aeolian mode over a **drone** of an open 5th, A–E, played by your partner on a keyboard or string instrument. (A drone is a note, or notes, of fixed pitch continuing throughout a section of music.)

Written activity

Set the following verses of 'A Red, Red Rose' by the eighteenth century Scottish poet Robert Burns to an eight-bar melody based on the Aeolian mode. (Each line will be one bar.) Your melody should move mainly in steps and consist of four two-bar phrases. The cadence points (rest points at the ends of phrases) should revolve around the first or fifth notes of the mode. (To achieve variety phrases can end on other notes.) The last phrase must end on the first note of the mode.

My luve is like a red, red rose,
That's newly sprung in June:
O my luve is like the melodie,
That's sweetly play'd in tune.

As fair art thou, my bonnie lass,
So deep in luve am I;
And I will luve thee still, my dear,
Till a' the seas gang dry.

A MOVIE THEME IN COMPOUND TIME TO PLAY

The 1970 film *Patton,* about the life of the famous World War II American commander General George Patton, won seven Oscars. Jerry Goldsmith composed its rousing musical score, the main theme of which is given below.

Patton Theme

Jerry Goldsmith

March tempo

'THE RAIDERS MARCH' (JOHN WILLIAMS)

from *RAIDERS OF THE LOST ARK*

Raiders of the Lost Ark, released in 1981, is one of the top ten box office films of all time. Produced by George Lucas and directed by Steven Spielberg, *Raiders* is a fantastic adventure which harks back to the old Saturday afternoon matinees and Hollywood B-grade movies popular in the 1930s and 1940s, as well as to the 'boys'-own' comics and adventure novels of the same era. It has all the elements that appeal to adolescents, including over-the-top action sequences; death-defying feats and cliff-hanging situations; exotic settings (it moves from the jungles of South America to the hinterlands of Tibet, the deserts of Egypt, a hidden submarine base, and an isolated island); the supernatural; sadistic Nazi villains; spiders and snakes; off-beat modes of transport (including horse-carts, biplanes, motorcycles, submarines, ships, horses, trains and trucks); and last but not least, an intrepid hero who survives crushings, shootings and burnings and who fears nothing except snakes!

As in *Star Wars*, the dramatic impact of the film is effectively heightened by the rousing orchestral score by John Williams. The famous theme 'The Raiders March' brilliantly captures the essence of the hero Indiana Jones with whom it is associated. Played by the huge London Symphony Orchestra, which appropriately gives a colourful, larger-than-life effect, the piece suggests a courageous, adventure-loving and all-conquering hero through its clever use of musical elements. In driving march time, it begins with an ostinato pattern whose rhythms are energetic and dynamic; the major-key melody contains many dotted rhythms and leaps, suggesting perhaps the hero's fondness for leaping into action; the timbre is dominated by the power and brilliance of the brass and percussion instruments; and the volume is loud to accompany Indy's noisy escapades.

The intrepid hero Indiana Jones (Harrison Ford) in a perilous situation

The main theme of 'The Raiders March' is given on page 52. Learn to play this 'leitmotiv' (as John Williams calls a theme that identifies a particular character), then listen to the piece following the piano score given in the *Score Book*. Note the use of musical elements to suggest the hero's character.

Raiders of the Lost Ark was awarded Oscars for Best Art Direction, Best Sound, Best Film Editing and Best Visual Effects. It was also nominated for Best Picture, Best Direction, Best Cinematography and Best Original Score.

'A piece like that is deceptively simple to try to find the few right notes that will make a right leitmotivic identification for a character like Indiana Jones. I remember working on that thing for days and days, changing notes, changing this, inverting that, trying to get something that seemed to me to be just right. I can't speak for my colleagues but for me things which appear to be very simple are not at all, they're only simple after the fact.

The manufacture of these things which seem inevitable is a process that can be laborious and difficult.'

**JOHN WILLIAMS
ON 'THE RAIDERS MARCH'**

THE BASIC PLOT
of *Raiders of the Lost Ark*

It is 1936 and Dr Indiana Jones (Harrison Ford), daredevil professor of archaeology, is hired by the US Government to find the Ark of the Covenant, the golden casket used by the ancient Hebrews to hold the Ten Commandments. The Ark is supposedly able to confer magical powers on the person who possesses it, being 'a radio for speaking to God', and contains an awesome destructive power. It is thus no surprise that Hitler is also after the Ark and that his agents are about to uncover it in a long-buried temple called the Well of Souls. Indy, together with his ex-girlfriend Marion Ravenwood (Karen Allen), are hot on their trail, and after surviving a never-ending series of perilous situations thwart the Nazis' efforts. The film ends with the villains receiving divine punishment for attempting to open the sacred Ark.

COMPOSER PROFILE

John Williams, born in the USA in 1932, began his career as a Hollywood composer by writing scores for episodes of the TV series *Wagon Train* and *Bachelor Father* in the 1950s, and *Gilligan's Island* in the 1960s. This led to work with the director and producer Irwin Allen on his science fiction shows, such as *Lost in Space* and *Land of the Giants,* in the 1960s and 1970s. His first critical movie success was his terrifying score for *Jaws* in 1975 which won him his first Oscar. This movie began his successful association with director Steven Spielberg with whom he has collaborated on ten films so far, including *Raiders of the Lost Ark* (1981), *E.T. The Extra-Terrestrial* (1982), *Schindler's List* (1993) and *Jurassic Park* (1993). His award-winning score for *Star Wars* in 1977 influenced other composers to write for large symphony orchestras. Williams, who has written for over 100 television shows and films, is considered by many to be the leading film composer writing today.

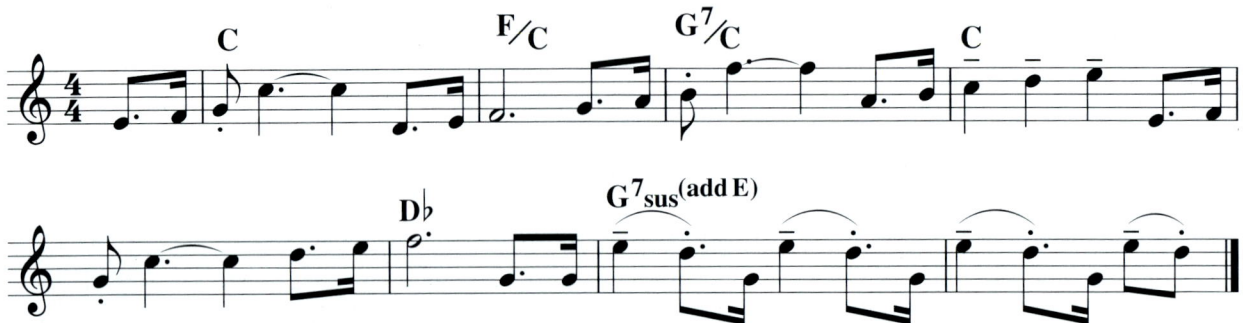

The Raiders March

John Williams

Note: The small lines placed above some of the notes are *tenuto* signs and indicate that the notes are to be held for their full value.

HARMONY

Chords and intervals

If you look at the piano score of 'The Raiders March' you will notice that most of the time the right hand plays **chords**, that is, two or more notes of different pitch sounding together. The chords used in bars 1–6 are two-note chords; in bars 7–9 some three-note chords are used, and in bars 25–32 there are several four-note chords. Not only can chords be made up of different numbers of notes, but these notes can also be arranged in different ways. Take for example bar 4, which uses all two-note chords. In the first chord the notes form the interval or distance in pitch of a 6th, if we count the letter names from the lower note E (counted as 1) to the upper note C (6). In the second chord the notes form the interval of a 5th and in the next three chords the notes form intervals of a 3rd. Listen to the sounds of these two-note chords as they are played to you.

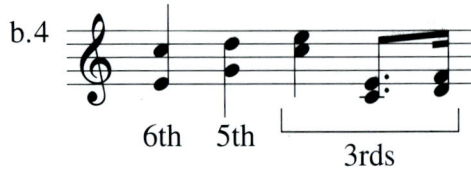

Now examine the three-note chords in bar 7. Each chord produces three intervals, consisting of the interval between: (1) the first and second notes; (2) the second and third notes; and (3) the first and third notes. For example, the first chord contains a 5th (F–C), a 3rd (C–E) and a 7th (F–E), while the second chord contains a 5th (F–C), a 2nd (C–D) and a 6th (F–D). Listen to these three-note chords as they are played to you.

Harmony, concords and discords

Another, more general term used for the chords in a piece of music is **harmony**. Harmony, like rhythm, melody and form, is a very important basic element of music, and can produce an emotional effect on the listener which the film composer can manipulate for various purposes, including the conveying of character. For an illustration of this, listen again to the harmonic effect produced by the chords of bar 5 as they are played to you. These chords are pleasant to the ear and seem to be at rest. They are what we call **concords**. Generally speaking, concords comprise the intervals of a 3rd, 4th, 5th, 6th and octave. Thus a composer wishing to picture a character at peace with the world would use mainly 'concordant' harmony.

Now listen again to the harmonic effect produced by the chords in bar 7. The chords are somewhat jarring on the ear and do not sound at rest. They are what we call **discords**. Generally speaking, chords containing the intervals of a 2nd and a 7th are discords. When any of these intervals are used within chords, as in bar 10, the whole chord is said to be 'discordant'. Some striking discords, intensified by accents, are used in bars 24–30. Listen as your teacher plays them and note their effect. To picture a character at odds with the world a composer would use discordant harmony. In 'The Raiders March', the frequent discords could perhaps picture the many conflicts that the hero has to face and overcome.

 ## Aural activities

1. Identify whether the chords played to you contain two or three notes.
2. Identify whether the chords played to you are concords or discords.

Triads

In bar 10 a very important three-note chord called a **triad** is used on beat 1.

   A triad is the most important kind of chord used in music and is the basis of most of our harmony. The lowest note of a triad is usually called the **root**; thus the other two notes are a 3rd and a 5th above the root. With your classmates, sing a triad to the solfa syllables doh, mi, soh.

 ## Written activities

1. Build triads on these root notes.

2. Find three other examples of triads in bars 12–23 of 'The Raiders March' and write them on a staff.

Chord symbols

Triads form the basis of the chords played by accompanying instruments such as guitars and autoharps. The particular triadic chords are indicated above the music by **chord symbols**, which are simply the letter names of the roots of the triads. In 'The Raiders March' score the chord symbols are above the right-hand staves. Note the following:

1. In bars 3 and 7 the G chord has a '7' written after it, indicating a **seventh chord**. This is a triad with an extra note, a seventh above the root, to add extra harmonic colour.
2. Some of the chord symbols have two letters separated by a stroke, for example F/C in bar 2. This indicates that the chord F is to be played by the right hand above a C bass note in the left hand. In some cases, when the bass note does not belong to the indicated chord (as in bars 3 and 10), striking discords are produced, which contribute to the particular dramatic effect desired by the composer (in this case the creation of tension).

 Written activity

Write the chords indicated by the chord symbols C, F, G and B♭.

Chromatic chords

Sometimes composers use chords containing **chromatic notes** or notes foreign to the key, as in bars 6 and 10 of 'The Raiders March' where the notes D♭ and B♭ are used respectively in C major. These chromatic notes produce **chromatic chords**, the effect of which can be surprising, colourful and, at times, quite dramatic. Once again the use of chromatic chords (because they are 'foreign' to the key) can produce a feeling of unrest and they are frequently used by film composers for various purposes, including the conveying of character. In 'The Raiders March' the chromatic chords reinforce the feeling of conflict faced by the hero. Can you find another example of a chromatic chord in the piece?

Pedal note

A **pedal note** provides another example of discordant or **dissonant harmony**. It is a long held or repeated bass note that does not always belong to the chords sounding above it. In bars 10–18 the repeated C bass note does not belong to the chords in bars 10, 12, 14, 16 and 18; therefore it produces dissonant harmony and the feeling of unrest. A C pedal note is also used in bars 1–5, producing dissonance in bar 3.

'MAIN TITLES' (RACHEL PORTMAN)

from *EMMA*

● *Gwyneth Paltrow as Emma and Jeremy Northam as Mr Knightly in the archery scene from Emma*

The 1996 film *Emma* is one of several recent films based on the novels of the nineteenth century English novelist Jane Austen. Set in the picturesque county of Sussex in England, it tells the story of the rather unsuccessful attempts at matchmaking by the beautiful young Emma Woodhouse on her unsuspecting friends. She is continually trying to unite friends who are utterly wrong for each other, while oblivious to her own feelings of love towards her long-time family friend, Mr Knightly.

The Oscar-winning musical score was composed and orchestrated by the young English composer Rachel Portman, one of the few female composers of film music at the present time. The score evokes a feeling of the English countryside with an almost exclusive use of woodwind and string instruments. The light-textured music with mainly solo use of woodwinds is appropriate for the intimate settings and Emma's small circle of friends. As befits the intimate nature of the film, Rachel Portman has written only a small number of themes, which are repeated throughout with variation. She has also based some of the music on modes that further help to evoke an English country setting.

The 'Main Titles' music introduces an important theme (given in the *Score Book*) which recurs throughout the film in many variations. The theme, in triple metre and in A major, has a lilting, folklike quality and comes to suggest the idea of love because of its repeated association with romantic events. For example it is heard when Emma dreams of the handsome Frank Churchill, when Mr Knightly tells Emma he is not in love with Jane Fairfax (a mutual acquaintance), and also when Mr Knightly finally proposes to Emma. In addition, the theme is used in the end titles when they marry.

The 'Main Titles' theme comprises two eight-bar sections, bars 1–8 and 17–24, that are repeated a number of times with small variations each time. These variations consist of slight changes of rhythm and added notes. Compare bars 1–8 with 9–16, 25–32 and 33–40, and compare bars 17–24 with 41–48 and 49–56. The theme is also varied through pitch, timbre (changes in instrumentation), texture, tempo and metre (the 'Main Titles' and 'End Titles' both contain a $\frac{6}{8}$ variation). Such variation is necessary to create variety and interest since the theme is used so frequently. Not only is it used at the beginning and at the end, the theme's constant use in different situations provides unity, binding the various scenes together.

Learn to play the first 24 bars of the 'Main Titles' theme transposed into C major on page 57. Then listen to the music, which is in two main sections, the first in a slow $\frac{3}{4}$, the second in a faster $\frac{6}{8}$. Follow the melody of the first section (given in the *Score Book*). After you have heard the 'Main Titles', listen again to the first section and identify the instruments playing the melody. Make a list of these, giving the bar numbers when they enter.

THE BASIC PLOT
of *Emma*

Emma Woodhouse (Gwyneth Paltrow), an upper-class young lady living in a small village in Sussex in the nineteenth century, acts as a matchmaker in trying to marry her young friend Harriet Smith (Toni Collette) to the Reverend Elton (Alan Cumming). Unfortunately Emma does not realise that Mr Elton is in love with her. When she rejects his advances he marries a wealthy and rather obnoxious lady from Bath. After unsuccessfully trying to match Harriet with a handsome newcomer, Emma discovers that Harriet has fallen in love with Mr Knightly (Jeremy Northam), Emma's greatest friend. She quickly comes to realise, however, that she herself loves Mr Knightly. After some misunderstandings the two are happily united. Harriet accepts the proposal of a young farmer with whom she was in love before Emma's ill-fated and meddling attempts at matchmaking.

COMPOSER PROFILE

Rachel Portman, born in 1960 in Haslemere, England, received her musical education at the University of Oxford. She began her composing career in the early 1980s and in 1988 won the British Film Institute's Young Composer of the Year award. She has written more than 30 film and television scores, including those for *Where Angels Fear to Tread* (1991), *The Joy Luck Club* (1993), the Australian film *Sirens* (1994) and *The Adventures of Pinocchio* (1996). For the score of *Emma* she won the 1996 Oscar for Best Musical/Comedy Score and created history by being the first female composer to win an Oscar for a film score. Portman orchestrates all of her scores herself (which is rare for film composers), and is highly regarded for her deep involvement with the characters and the drama of the films that she underscores.

'Main Titles' theme from Emma

Rachel Portman

Slow and free

Written activity

Write two variations on the melody given below. You may like to alter the rhythm, add extra notes or even change the metre.

'OF FOREIGN LANDS AND PEOPLE'

from *MY BRILLIANT CAREER*   (ROBERT SCHUMANN)

► *Judy Davis as Sybylla Melvyn and Sam Neill as Harry Beecham in the garden of Harry's home in* My Brilliant Career

THE BASIC PLOT
of *My Brilliant Career*

In 1897, in the middle of a drought, Sybylla Melvyn (Judy Davis) is living with her poverty-stricken family on their cattle property in outback Australia. Her parents do not know how to manage a daughter who wants to do great things—have her own career in literature, music or art and meet creative people who have visions—rather than marry, as was customary, and be supported by a husband. Sybylla is sent to stay with her wealthy grandmother to learn manners and social graces, and falls in love with a young neighbouring landowner, Harry Beecham (Sam Neill). He finds her independence appealing but her behaviour not ideal. Still dreaming of an artistic future, Sybylla is sent to teach a poor family of unruly children in order to repay a debt of her father's. Harry finally proposes and Sybylla must decide between less-than-perfect love and independence. She asks for time to fulfil her dream.

The Australian author Miles Franklin, born in 1879, was raised on an isolated station in the outback and at the age of 16 wrote a novel about her life entitled *My Brilliant Career*. Six years later this novel was published in Edinburgh. In 1979, 100 years after Miles Franklin's birth, a group of Australian women film-makers turned the novel into a remarkable film telling the story of a restless, high-spirited, independent young woman, Sybylla Melvyn, whose unconventional behaviour was not considered at all suitable in the late Victorian era (at the end of the nineteenth century). The film, which won seven Australian Film Institute Awards in 1979 and two British Academy Awards in 1981 (including Best Actress for Judy Davis), traces Sybylla's life of poverty at home, her visit to her wealthy grandmother, her falling in love, her difficult teaching experiences with a poor family and her final choice between love and a career as a writer.

Up till now the music we have studied, except 'The Entertainer' and 'The Turkish March', has been specifically composed for the particular film in which it features.

Frequently, however, directors select music that has already been composed to evoke time and place, convey character or ideas, to create a mood or atmosphere or to express emotions in their films. One such example is 'Of Foreign Lands and People' from *Scenes of Childhood* by the German romantic period composer Robert Schumann (1810–56), chosen to convey the main character's dream of liberation. The choice of this classical piece is appropriate because Sybylla is an excellent young pianist with a passion for the arts.

As she plays the plaintive melody and constant, restless quaver triplet rhythms the music vividly portrays her yearning for a more satisfying life and her dreams of doing great things and meeting interesting and imaginative people. The contour of the phrase melodies in bars 1–8 and 15–22, with a leap upwards from B to G followed by descending steps, reinforces the idea of Sybylla's yearning, while the chromatic chord on beat 2 of bars 1, 3, 15 and 17 adds to the pathos. The music occurs on a number of occasions in the film, the timbre each time matching the setting. At the beginning Sybylla is playing on a 'tinny'-sounding old farmhouse piano. Later, when she is in a more ladylike situation at her grandmother's home the music is orchestrated for **string quartet**, a group made up of two violins, viola and cello, which at the time was considered suitable entertainment for the upper class. At the end of the film we see Sybylla leaving her neat cottage and carrying a parcel addressed to her publisher in Scotland. As the new day begins she leans on the gate and seems to gaze into the future. The piece is again heard, with the piano joined by the string quartet for a rich, full sound seeming to imply a future of great promise.

Learn to play the melody of 'Of Foreign Lands and People' given on page 60 and then listen to the music, which is in binary form (AB), while following the score in the *Score Book*. Study the music and note:

1. the way the quaver triplets are divided between the hands, the left hand playing the first two quavers and the right hand playing the third quaver;
2. the indications for the sustaining pedal underneath the left-hand part;
3. the **sequence**—repetition of a pattern at a different pitch level—in bars 9–10 and 11–12;
4. the dynamic markings—*mf*, *p* and $>$ $<$ (**dynamics** are the degrees of loudness or softness indicated by terms and signs in the score);
5. the tempo indications written in the music—*rit.*, *ritardando*, *a tempo* and *poco rall.*

COMPOSER PROFILE

Robert Schumann (1810–56) was an important German Romantic composer of the nineteenth century who excelled in writing short piano pieces, which were frequently organised into sets and given imaginative titles such as *Scenes of Childhood*, *Carnival* and *Fantasy Pieces*. His music is very expressive, ranging from lyrical (songlike and dreamy) to dramatic. His *Scenes of Childhood* (to which 'Of Foreign Lands and People' belongs) was composed in 1838 and comprises 13 short programmatic pieces for piano filled with childlike innocence.

Of Foreign Lands and People

Robert Schumann

Score reading activity

Study the score of 'Of Foreign Lands and People' and do the following:

1. Name the key of the music. (Give two reasons for your answer.)
2. Describe the time signature and state what it means.
3. Write the letter names of the left-hand quavers with stems going down for bars 3–8.
4. Name the curved line above bars 1 and 2 and state what it means.
5. Name the curved line in the final bar and state what it means.
6. Name the sign ⌒ in bar 14 and state what it means.
7. Name the sign at the end of bar 8 :‖ and state what it means.
8. Give the Italian word and its meaning for each of the four dynamic markings.
9. Give the Italian word and its meaning for each of the four tempo indications.
10. Give the letter names of the notes of the minim chord played by the right and left hands in the final bar. What special chord do these notes form?

 ## Practical activity

Play 'Soldier's March' by Robert Schumann in the *Score Book*.

FILM MUSIC FOR AURAL ANALYSIS

Listen to 'The Gremlin Rag' from *Gremlins*, which depicts two contrasting types of character. The music is by the American composer Jerry Goldsmith, who has written more than 200 popular scores for film and television. Explain how the composer depicts and contrasts the characters through musical elements such as rhythm, melodic **range** (the distance between the highest and lowest notes) and contour, timbre, texture, tempo, dynamics and **articulation** (the attack or release of the notes). A brief background is given for the film so that you will understand the characters portrayed by the music.

'The Gremlin Rag' (Jerry Goldsmith)

from *Gremlins*

The 1984 comic horror film *Gremlins* has the distinction of being one of the top ten grossing films of all time. It tells the story of a cute, furry pet called Gizmo which is given to an American teenager as a Christmas gift. Because the boy disobeys the rules about looking after the mysterious but lovable 'mogwai', it produces a huge number of murderous off-spring—the little green 'gremlins' whose sole aim is to destroy the local town and all the people in it.

The film has a most effective score by Jerry Goldsmith, one of the leading film composers since the 1960s, who ranks with such other successful modern composers as John Williams and John Barry. Goldsmith set out to write themes for both the mogwai Gizmo and its evil progeny the gremlins that would show their contrasting natures: the gentle and lovable character of the former and the nasty and repulsive character of the latter. In 'The Gremlin Rag' Gizmo's theme is heard first, followed by the music for the Gremlins.

Activities for senior students

Composition

Imagine you are writing music for a film involving two contrasting main characters. Write personality profiles for them and then write musical themes to convey their character. Harmonise and arrange your music for appropriate instruments. Consider such elements as contour (steps/leaps), rhythm, tonality/modality, harmony, consonance/dissonance, timbre and texture.

Arranging

Select a piece of film music that portrays character, for example 'The Raiders March', and arrange it for available instruments, ensuring that your orchestration contributes to the portrayal of character.

Create a soundtrack

Select an appropriate piece of recorded music to depict a particular character on film. Dub the music onto the film.

Research activity

Find three films for which the music was written by John Williams—for example, *Star Wars*, *Superman* and *E.T. the Extra-Terrestrial*—and discuss how character is conveyed through the music. You will need to quote the musical themes to which you are referring and to analyse them, relating their musical elements to the particular characters.

Oral presentation

Using video excerpts provide an interpretation and analysis of the music of a film to depict character, for example *The Return of the Jedi*. Compare and contrast the themes given to each character, discussing how the musical elements help to portray them.

WORDS TO KNOW

melodic ostinato	compound triple
interval	compound
semitone	quadruple
tone	Mixolydian mode
swing	drone
sharp	chord
flat	harmony
natural	concord
chromatic scale	discord
whole-tone scale	triad
military band	root
style	chord symbol
triplet	seventh chord
word painting	chromatic note
major scale	chromatic chord
scale degrees	pedal note
key	dissonant
accidental	harmony
key signature	string quartet
A natural minor	sequence
scale	dynamics
Aeolian mode	range
compound time	articulation
compound duple	

Section 3

The 1975 Australian film Picnic at Hanging Rock, about three school girls and their teacher who mysteriously disappear during a school excursion, used the haunting sounds of the panpipes to create an eerie, unsettled mood

CREATING A MOOD OR ATMOSPHERE

One of the most important functions of film music is to create a mood or atmosphere so as to prepare an audience for what they are about to see; or, to put it another way, to create an aural frame of reference for viewing the visual images. This means that the music must perfectly complement the mood created by the on-screen elements—the size, shape, colour, brightness and texture of the images, their speed of movement, the physical qualities of the background, and so on. For example, to accompany a scene set in outer space a composer would probably write music with a wide range of sounds—from very low to very high—to match the vastness of space; to accompany a desert scene the music would probably feature high-pitched discordant sounds to emphasise the harshness and heat of the sun's rays.

Sometimes the timbre of an instrument or group of instruments can be exploited to create a mood, for example lower strings to create a dark mood; or a style of music can create a mood, such as heavy rock for a harsh, brutal effect.

The music played at the very beginning of a film, often under the credits if they occur there, not only puts us in the right frame of mind to see the film but also gives us clues as to its essential nature. Thus a comedy film will have light-hearted music and a horror film will have tense, scary music. (Sometimes of course a cunning director of a horror movie can fool us by beginning with light-hearted music to create a false impression; this makes the sudden 'shock'—accompanied by appropriately dramatic music—all the more effective.) Let us begin this section with a very famous example of opening mood-creating music.

'ROCK AROUND THE CLOCK'

from *BLACKBOARD JUNGLE*

(Words and music by MAX C. FREEMAN and JIMMY DE KNIGHT, performed by BILL HALEY AND THE COMETS)

NORTH MANUAL HIGH SCHOOL

▲ *Glen Ford as the idealistic teacher Rick Dadier observes his rebellious students at play*

Blackboard Jungle, with its realistic portrayal of teenage rebellion in the classroom, caused a storm of controversy when it appeared in 1955. Many accused the film of provoking violence and one critic labelled it as communist propaganda. Though fairly tame by today's standards, it is best remembered for the fact that it was the first film to use rock music in its soundtrack.

During the opening credits, the song 'Rock around the Clock', performed by the group Bill Haley and the Comets, is used to set the tone for the underlying theme of rebellion. For the time, it was an inspired choice by director Richard Brooks, as the style of the song, **rock 'n' roll,** symbolised to the parents of the mid 1950s a contempt for authority and a rejection of traditional white, middle-class values.

The rock 'n' roll style was performed by small instrumental groups consisting of amplified acoustic guitars, double bass, saxophone and drums, and was characterised by a frenzied, raucous sound and a strong beat for dancing. The songs had simple lyrics on simple subject matter (often to do with dancing) and were based on three primary-triad chords (see the following page). The general mood of rock 'n' roll was liberation and fun—qualities that perfectly match the mood of the New York delinquent students portrayed in *Blackboard Jungle.*

Listen to 'Rock around the Clock' while following the music in the *Score Book* and noting the mood created by the rock 'n' roll style.

THE BASIC PLOT
of *Blackboard Jungle*

The idealistic, middle-aged teacher Rick Dadier (Glenn Ford) is sent to a tough Manhattan inner-city school. Nicknamed 'Daddy-O' by his rebellious class of teenage boys, he tries to get through to his students despite their hostile and violent resistance, and the opposition of the ineffectual school administration. He is able to win over a black student (Sidney Poitier) but the top hoodlum, Artie West (Vic Morrow), refuses to cooperate. When the threats against Dadier extend to his pregnant wife (Anne Francis), Dadier is forced to stand up to Artie and challenge his hold over the other boys. At first aligning themselves to their gang leader, the boys increasingly gain respect for their new teacher and gradually come over to his side.

Practical activities

1. Perform the chorus melody of 'Rock around the Clock' in the *Score Book* with chordal accompaniment.
2. Perform 'Blue Suede Shoes' on page 67 with chordal accompaniment.
3. Sing the rock 'n' roll songs in the *Score Book*.

Primary triads

Most rock 'n' roll songs (including 'Rock around the Clock' and 'Blue Suede Shoes') are based on only three chords: those built on the first, fourth and fifth degrees of the major scale. For 'Rock around the Clock' these chords, written as triads, are as follows:

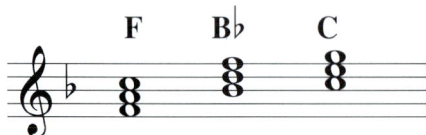

These particular triads are called **primary triads** because they are the most important triads.

Triads can also be indicated by Roman numerals:

1. The primary triad built on the first degree of the scale is I.
2. The primary triad built on the fourth degree of the scale is IV.
3. The primary triad built on the fifth degree of the scale is V.

PERFORMER PROFILE

Bill Haley (1927–81), originally a cowboy singer, became famous in the early 1950s when his group Bill Haley and the Comets began recording rhythm and blues songs. 'Rock around the Clock', in the new rock 'n' roll style, was only a moderate hit when first released in 1954, but its follow-up, the band's version of Big Joe Turner's 'Shake, Rattle and Roll' sold a million copies. Helped by its use in *Blackboard Jungle*, 'Rock around the Clock' was rereleased in 1955 and achieved enormous popularity (25 million in record sales worldwide). The song quickly became a kind of anthem for young people rebelling against the values of the older generation. Haley's pudgy, balding appearance did not lend itself to teen idol status and by 1957 his career was in decline.

A ROCK 'N' ROLL TUNE TO PLAY

The most famous rock 'n' roll artist of all, Elvis Presley, starred in a string of hit musical films during the 1960s and 1970s. An early film, *G.I. Blues* (1960), featured the singer as a raw American army recruit, or 'G.I.', sent to Germany. 'Blue Suede Shoes' was one of the songs featured. It is sung to a 'shuffle' rhythm (where ti-tis are performed more as tim-kas) and has the time signature ₵ indicating two minim beats to the bar.

Blue Suede Shoes

Carl Lee Perkins

Written activities

1. Write the primary triads indicated by the chord symbols above the music given below. (Remember that the letter of the chord symbol is the root of the triad.) There should be four crotchets per bar except in the final bar, which should have a dotted minim triad to match the melody. The first bar is given as an example.

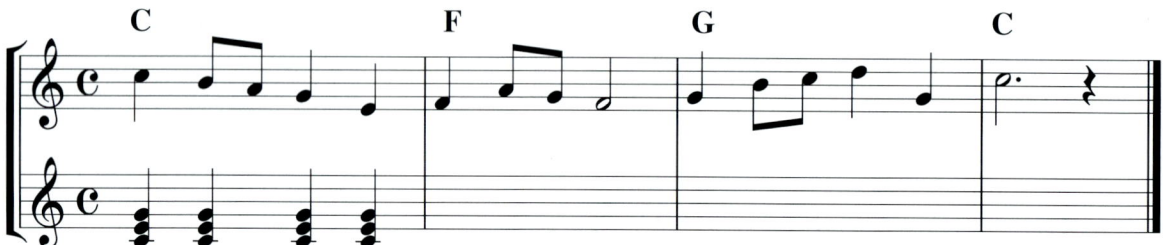

2. Write the triads indicated by the chord symbols. For bars 2 and 3 follow the rhythmic pattern of the triads given in bar 1. Match the note value in the last bar with that of the melody.

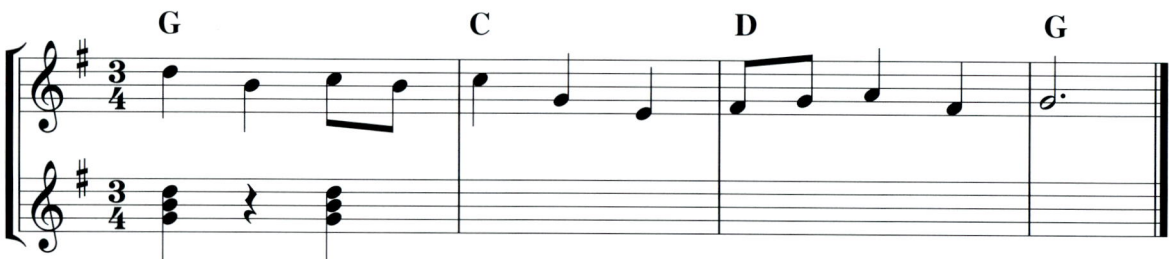

3. Work out the chord symbols to indicate the given triads, and write the symbols in the correct positions. *Note*: A new chord symbol is used only when the triad changes.

Aural activity

In your manuscript books, draw bar lines to make eight blank bars. Your teacher will then play an eight-bar melody accompanied by chords I and V. Listen to it carefully, and identify the chords used. Write either I or V in each corresponding blank bar. When you can successfully identify chords I and V your teacher will add chord IV.

BLUES PROGRESSION

The primary triads used in 'Rock around the Clock' form a particular 12-bar arrangement of chords, or **chord progression**, found in many rock 'n' roll songs. This is known as the **blues chord progression** and can be represented by chord symbols or Roman numerals. For example, the blues chord progression used in 'Rock around the Clock' in both chord symbols and Roman numerals is as follows:

F | F | F | F | I | I | I | I |

B♭| B♭| F | F | IV | IV | I | I |

C | C | F | F ‖   V | V | I | I ‖

The blues progression in G is used for the first 12 bars of 'Blue Suede Shoes'. (Note the use of seventh chords in bars 4, 5–6 and 9–10 as well as in bar 12 to add extra harmonic colour.)

 Practical and **Written activities**

1. Write the 12-bar blues progression in C major using chord symbols. Play the progression on autoharp, guitar or keyboard as you sing 'Rock around the Clock'.
2. Write the blues progression used in the first 12 bars of 'Blue Suede Shoes'. The chord symbols are indicated above the music. (Include the seventh chords.) Play the progression as others play the melody.
3. Write the primary triads in C major, G major, D major and B flat major. First write the key signature and then the three primary triads in that key. Add the corresponding Roman numeral under each triad.
4. Write your own rock 'n' roll song. Both the verse and the chorus should be based on a blues progression or a variation of it. Arrange your song for performance with accompaniment on keyboard/guitar, bass and drums. (You will need to research the characteristic rhythms and bass lines of rock 'n' roll.)

SETTING COUPLETS IN SIMPLE TIME

A **couplet** is two lines of verse. The lyrics of many songs are made up of couplets; for example, if you look at the words of the first verse of 'Be-Bop-A-Lula' in the *Score Book*, you will notice that it is made up of two rhyming couplets:

She's the girl in the red blue jeans,
She's the queen of all the teens.
She's the one that I know,
She's the one that loves me so.

The rhythmic pattern for a couplet usually has four accents per line and can be set as either eight bars of $\frac{2}{4}$ or $\frac{3}{4}$ time or four bars of $\frac{4}{4}$ time, as in 'Be-Bop-A-Lula'.

Setting couplets to rhythmic patterns is the first step in learning how to write a song. Revise 'Setting words to rhythms' on page 29 then do the written activities on page 70.

Written activities

1. Set the following couplets to rhythmic patterns as indicated. Note that the second couplet in each metre begins with an anacrusis.

   (a) *Duple metre, eight bars long:*

       (i) Pat-a cake, pat-a cake, baker's man,
           Bake me a cake as fast as you can.

       (ii) The maid was in the garden hanging out the clothes,
           When down came a blackbird and pecked off her nose.

   (b) *Triple metre, eight bars long:*

       (i) Little Boy Blue come blow your horn,
           The sheep's in the meadow, the cow's in the corn.

       (ii) So leave your supper and leave your sleep
           And come with your playfellows down the street.

   (c) *Quadruple metre, four bars long:*

       (i) Where are you going to, my pretty maid?
           I'm going a-milking, Sir, she said.

       (ii) I had a little nut tree and nothing would it bear,
           But a silver nutmeg and a golden pear.

2. Set the following couplets to rhythmic patterns as indicated. In these couplets there will be only three accented syllables in the second line. In $\frac{2}{4}$ or $\frac{3}{4}$ time this will require a note tied across the bar line between the last two bars, and in $\frac{4}{4}$ time it will require a long note or rests.

   (a) *Duple metre, eight bars long:*

           Little Jack Horner sat in the corner
           Eating his Christmas pie.

   (b) *Triple metre, eight bars long:*

           The little dog laughed to see such fun
           And the dish ran away with the spoon.

   (c) *Quadruple metre, four bars long:*

           Old Mother Hubbard went to the cupboard
           To fetch her poor dog a bone.

'BABY ELEPHANT WALK' (HENRY MANCINI)

from *HATARI*

Δ *John Wayne as Sean Mercer and his friends watch in bemused surprised as one of the baby elephants runs through a shop in a scene from* Hatari

*H*atari (1962), set in Tanganyika, the present-day United Republic of Tanzania, is a light-hearted adventure film about trapping African animals for zoos. Although the film features some well-known Hollywood actors of the time, including John Wayne, it is the animals that are the real stars. Much of the film is taken up with exciting and realistic game-hunting sequences that depict the beauty, speed and ferocity of the animals of the Tanganyika plains. The hunters are frequently in dangerous situations; in fact the word 'Hatari' means danger in Swahili, the native language of the Bantu people of the coastal areas of Tanganyika.

A notable aspect of the film is Henry Mancini's score, including novelty pieces such as 'Baby Elephant Walk' which captures the playful, light-hearted nature of the three baby elephants featured in the film. It is heard when the freelance photographer Dallas decides to take the little elephants for a swim. They trot along behind her down to the large waterhole and there they frolic, gurgle and roll in the water. The music, with its jaunty rhythms and jazz elements, creates the necessary cheerful mood for the scene.

'Baby Elephant Walk', in F major, features a one-bar ostinato pattern in the bass, played staccato on organ, which changes pitch according to the blues chord progression and is heard almost throughout the piece. This ostinato gives the impression of the little elephants trotting along.

The form of the piece is a blues, that is, it uses the 12-bar blues chord progression (see page 69). In bar 10 chord IV is used instead of chord V—a common variation. The progression is heard five times, each playing comprising one **chorus**. In jazz, **chorus form** is the term applied to pieces that use the choruses of popular songs as the basis of variation and improvisation. In 'Baby Elephant Walk' each chorus has different instrumentation, and two choruses feature improvisation.

Another important jazz element found in 'Baby Elephant Walk' is the use of **blue notes**. These notes, which originated in African-American vocal blues songs of the nineteenth century, are produced by flattening the third, fifth and seventh degrees of the major scale, as shown below.

These blue notes appear throughout, sometimes disguised by different letter names and accidentals. For example, the G in bar 1 in the bass is actually A♭, the flattened 3rd; and B♮ in bar 6 in the right hand is actually C♭, the flattened 5th.

Also contributing to the comical mood are the unusual timbral effects from such instruments as muted brass, pipe organ and shrill clarinet, as well as the slides and growls on the brass.

Listen to 'Baby Elephant Walk' following the first page of the piano score in the *Score Book*. Read the listening outline and listen again to the piece.

THE BASIC PLOT
of *Hatari*

Sean Mercer (John Wayne), is the leader of a group of professional hunters engaged in trapping animals for zoos. He falls in love with Dallas (Elsa Martinelli), a beautiful freelance photographer, while three of the other hunters compete for the affections of Brandy (Michèle Girardon), the youthful owner of a game farm. Against Sean's wishes, Dallas adopts and rears three orphaned baby elephants. Thinking Sean does not love her, she leaves the game farm but is tracked down by the three little elephants and reunited with Sean for a happy ending.

COMPOSER PROFILE

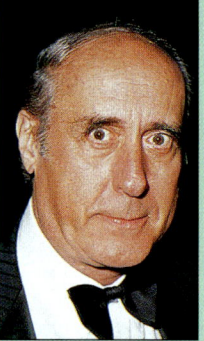

American Henry Mancini (1924–94) began his career as a composer writing jazz arrangements for the band leader Benny Goodman. During the 1950s at Universal Studios he composed the music for many films, including *The Glenn Miller Story* (1954), helping to change the style of film music from traditional orchestral to jazz-inspired. Mancini won numerous awards, including four Oscars, 20 Grammys and two Emmys. He recorded over 50 albums and had 500 works published. His most famous film music is the 'Theme' from *The Pink Panther*.

Listening outline

Introduction .. Short ascending and descending passage on organ followed by six bars of the organ ostinato given earlier, based on chord I

Chorus 1 ...... Cheerful clarinet melody with staccato articulation, semitone 'slides' and blue notes

Four-bar link .. Ostinato with added spiky muted brass chords

Chorus 2 ...... Melody played by sparkling piccolo and glockenspiel with low brass growls

Chorus 3 ...... First four bars feature call-and-response between brass and organ; followed by eight bars of alto saxophone improvisation, adding to the feeling of playful freedom

Chorus 4 ...... First four bars as for Chorus 3 followed by eight bars of flute improvisation

Four-bar link .. Ostinato pattern

Chorus 5 ...... As for Chorus 1 but with full band from bar 9 and two extra bars inserted between bars 10 and 11

Tag (Coda) .. Short phrase played slowly on organ

 ## Practical activities

1. In 'Baby Elephant Walk' Choruses 3 and 4 featured improvisation over the blues progression. Using the notes given below in C, F and G majors (some of which are blue notes), improvise simple four-bar phrases while your classmates play the corresponding blues progression. You may use either the underlying rock 'n' roll 'shuffle' rhythm or 'straight' quavers as in 'Baby Elephant Walk'.

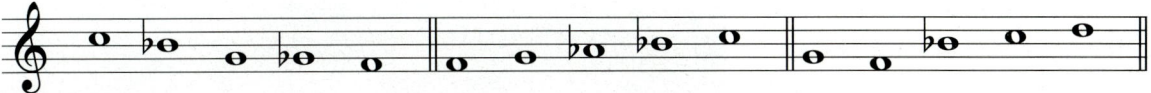

2. **Using the notes of the full blues scale (see previous page) improvise melodic phrases to blues progressions in various keys.**

'RIVER' AND 'GABRIEL'S OBOE'

from *THE MISSION*   (ENNIO MORRICONE)

The 1986 film *The Mission* tells the story of the attempt of Jesuit priests, led by Father Gabriel, to bring Christianity to the Indians of South America during the eighteenth century. Set in the jungles of Brazil, the film boasts spectacular photography—especially of the Iguaçu Falls, near which the Jesuit mission is established—and a wonderful musical score by the leading Italian film composer Ennio Morricone. Morricone subtly evokes a feeling of time and place, through the use of musical styles appropriate to the two different cultural groups featured in the film (the indigenous South Americans and the eighteenth century Europeans) and through the use of particular instruments characteristic of these styles, such as panpipes, *quena* (a kind of bamboo flute) and conga drums for the Indians, and oboe and harpsichord for the Europeans. (A harpsichord, pictured on page 75, is a keyboard instrument whose strings are plucked by quills to give a bright and brittle sound.)

Music in *The Mission* is used to create moods appropriate to the various dramatic situations as they unfold. Two very effective mood pieces are 'River', used during the Portuguese attack on the Indians, and 'Gabriel's Oboe', associated with Father Gabriel and his mission of love and peace. Heard separately at first, the two themes are later combined to symbolise the embracing of Christianity by the Indians.

'River'

'River', in D major and simple triple metre, creates a dramatic and unsettled mood as the noble Indians prepare to battle for their very existence. Features contributing to the mood include the *andante* tempo (an easy walking pace), and the use of a choir singing in harmony accompanied by strings, horns and timpani, as well as by conga drums and quena, giving an authentic sound. The music is dynamic and vigorous, with staccato articulation on beats 1 and 3 and tenuto on beat 2. An impression of constant movement is achieved by the steady, mainly crotchet, beat, the repeated chords, the continual semiquaver patterns on conga drums, the five-bar bass ostinato, and the repetition of a five-bar harmonised phrase above the bass.

The music is marked by a fast **harmonic rhythm** of primary triads, that is, the chords change frequently, providing forward motion. Other elements that progressively change are the dynamics and the pitch, both of which rise to an impressive and inspiring climax.

Listen to 'River' following the piano score in the *Score Book* and noting how the composer creates the dramatic and unsettled mood.

▼ *The spectacular Iguaçu Falls, Brazil, featured in* The Mission

'Gabriel's Oboe'

'Gabriel's Oboe', also in D major, and introduced by timpani, is first played by Father Gabriel during a tense situation in the rainforest above the waterfall. Through his gentle music and the sad and tranquil sound of the oboe, he tries to charm the Indians hidden in the trees and convince them he has come in peace. The peaceful mood of the expressive oboe solo, heard later accompanied by strings and harpsichord, is created by the *adagio* tempo (slow), frequent step-wise movement of the notes and soft dynamics. When the melody is repeated, a **counter melody** on strings is heard, providing variety. (A counter melody is a second melody played against the first.) A striking feature of the oboe melody is the use of semiquaver patterns moving in steps to 'decorate' it. (This **ornamentation** was a common practice in music of the eighteenth century.) As the pitch of the music gradually ascends to a high B, it seems to express a sublime hope and triumph over adversity.

Listen to 'Gabriel's Oboe' following the piano score in the *Score Book* and noting how the composer creates the peaceful mood.

THE BASIC PLOT of *The Mission*

In the eighteenth century, Jesuit priests, led by Father Gabriel (Jeremy Irons), attempt to bring Christianity to the Indians in the Amazonian jungles of Brazil. They set up a successful mission above the spectacular Iguaçu Falls but run into opposition from the Spanish and Portuguese colonial powers who are intent on capturing the Indians for slaves and on plundering the region's natural resources. Meanwhile, the slave dealer Mendoza (Robert De Niro) kills his brother in a fit of jealous rage but is prevented by Father Gabriel from committing suicide. After doing penance by climbing a cliff while dragging a heavy weight made of armour, Mendoza finds peace, becomes a priest and takes an active role in the running of the harmonious mission above the falls. However, the Catholic Church, under political pressure from Europe, cedes the land to the Portuguese, allowing the slave traders to return. Breaking his vows and ignoring the wishes of Father Gabriel, Mendoza helps the Indians to mount an armed resistance. Inevitably, both the priests and the Indians meet a violent and bloody end.

COMPOSER PROFILE

Italian composer Ennio Morricone (born 1928) is the most successful and prolific European film composer alive today. He has written for over 350 films, both European and American, and is known for his versatility in being able to compose effective scores and songs for a wide range of films, such as dramas, comedies, westerns, thrillers and epic spectacles. His many successful achievements include *A Fistful of Dollars* (1964), *The Good, the Bad and the Ugly* (1966), *Exorcist II: The Heretic* (1977), *The Untouchables* (1987) and *Wolf* (1994). Morricone has received four Academy Award nominations, and in 1996 he was honoured by the Society for the Preservation of Film Music with its Career Achievement Award, in recognition of his immeasurable impact on films and film music over his 35-year career.

▲ *A harpsichord as heard in 'Gabriel's Oboe'*

Practical activity

Play the melody of 'Falls' from *The Mission* given in the *Score Book*. Begin at bar 6. Keyboard players should play the whole piece as an accompaniment.

 Written and **Practical activity**

Arrange 'River' for tuned and untuned instruments available in your classroom. Conduct the class as they perform your arrangement.

MAJOR AND PERFECT INTERVALS

The melodies of 'River', 'Gabriel's Oboe' and 'Falls', like most melodies, are made up of steps, leaps and repeated notes. In music we refer to these as intervals, an interval being the difference in pitch between two notes. You have already encountered the interval of an octave, the difference of eight letter-names. If we take one octave of the C major scale and number each note with its corresponding scale degree number, we can determine the size of each interval above C. For example, D, the second note of the scale, is the interval of a 2nd above C. Similarly, G, the fifth note of the scale, is the interval of a 5th above C.

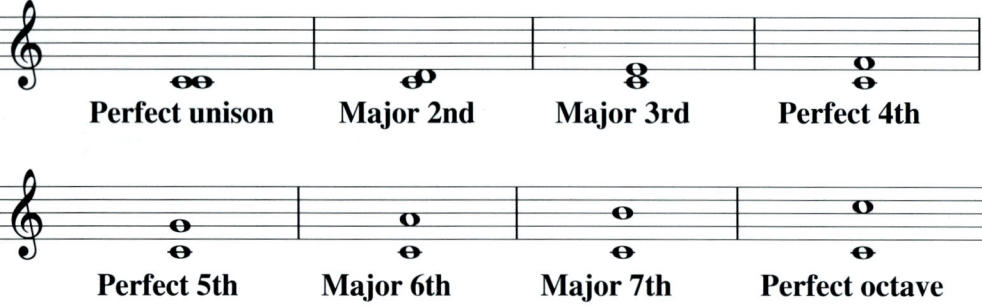

Work out the intervals between the following notes:

C–E .... C–F .... C–A .... C–B ....

In addition to working out the size of an interval we must also determine its quality. In a major scale, intervals are either major or perfect. Study the following intervals, which use the notes of the C major scale.

Perfect unison	Major 2nd	Major 3rd	Perfect 4th

Perfect 5th	Major 6th	Major 7th	Perfect octave

In a major scale, the **perfect intervals** are the **unison** (both notes the same pitch), the 4th, 5th and octave. The **major intervals** are the 2nd, 3rd, 6th and 7th. Listen as your teacher plays the major and perfect intervals given above and note their differences.

Major and perfect intervals can be sung using solfege, as follows:

> major 2nd—doh-mi, mi-re, fa-soh, soh-lah
> major 3rd—doh-mi, fa-la, soh-ti
> perfect 4th—doh-fa, re-soh, mi-la, soh-doh[1]
> perfect 5th—doh-soh, re-la, mi-ti, fa-doh[1]
> major 6th—doh-la, re-ti
> major 7th—doh-ti
> perfect 8ve—doh-doh[1]

Note: In music there are two ways of thinking about intervals. We can measure the distance in pitch between two successive notes of a melody in which the intervals move horizontally, such as D–F♯ in bar 6 of the 'Falls' melody in the *Score Book*; we can also measure the interval vertically if the notes are written one above the other in a chord, such as G–B in the right-hand part of bar 1 or G–D in the left-hand part of bar 6.

So far we have examined only intervals above C, which we regarded as the key note of the scale in which the intervals occurred. To measure the interval above a note other than C, we must think of the lower note of the two as the key note of the scale in which the interval occurs. The intervals below have G as their lower note; therefore, G becomes the key note of the scale in which they occur. Name the intervals correctly. The first two have been named for you.

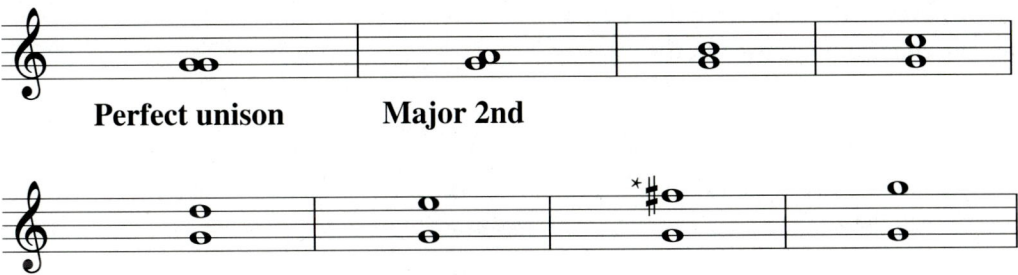

Perfect unison   Major 2nd

* Note the F♯ which belongs to the G major scale.

 ## Written activities

1. Name the intervals given below.

2. Write the notes to form the required intervals above A.

Major 6th   Perfect 4th   Major 2nd   Major 7th   Major 3rd

3. In the music of 'Falls' in the *Score Book* you will find six **pairs of successive notes with brackets above or below them** ⌐ and four vertical pairs of notes with brackets beside them]. Name each interval correctly.

 ## Aural activity

Identify the intervals played to you according to their size and quality.

 ## Practical activity

Sing a variety of songs that contain the major and perfect intervals you have just studied.

SIMPLE MELODY WRITING

Chordal and non-chordal notes

The melody used in 'River' is unusual because it is made up entirely of **chordal notes,** that is, notes that belong to the indicated chords. Given below for you to study is the melody of bars 1 and 2 with the notes of the chords written out in full above the music. The chordal notes used in the melody are circled.

In 'Gabriel's Oboe' the melody consists of chordal notes and **non-chordal notes,** that is, notes that do not belong to the indicated chords. Given below for you to study is the melody of bars 1 and 2 with the notes of the chords written out in full above the music. The non-chordal notes are circled on the music.

Most melodies contain a mixture of chordal and non-chordal notes. You will notice from 'Gabriel's Oboe' that most of the non-chordal notes are a step away on either side from chordal notes. The only leaps in the melody are to, or away from, chordal notes.

Play the following melodies and identify the non-chordal notes in each melody.

Writing a simple four-bar melody

The melody of 'River' is based on primary triads, as are many other well-known melodies. Let us use the primary triads to write a simple four-bar melody using one chord per bar. One possible chord progression would be I–IV–V–I. The process for writing a satisfactory melody to this chord progression is summarised in the following guidelines. After you have read the guidelines, study the 'Sample four-bar melody'. Play the melody with chordal accompaniment.

1. Use chordal notes on the strong beats of the bar (the first beat in duple and triple metre, the first and third beats in quadruple metre).
2. Non-chordal notes may be used for other notes provided they are just a step away from a note on either side.

3. Always end on the **tonic**, the first degree of the scale.
4. Avoid large leaps as they are hard to sing. Remember that you only leap to, or away from, chordal notes.
5. Make the range at least a 6th but not more than a 9th (one more than an octave).
6. The **leading note** is the seventh degree of the scale and must always be followed by the tonic *above* it in the next bar.
7. If a melody begins with an anacrusis, it should be one of the notes of chord V, preferably the **dominant**, that is, the fifth degree of the scale.
8. A good melody will have a mixture of steps and leaps to make an interesting contour or shape.

Sample four-bar melody

Aural activity

Listen to the four melodies played to you. One melody has too narrow a range, one has too wide a range, one has too many steps, and one has too many leaps. Explain what is wrong with each melody.

 Written and **Practical activities**

1. The melody above contains a number of mistakes, according to the guidelines. Listen to it as it is played with the accompaniment indicated by the chord symbols. Then do the following:

   (a) Write the letter names of the chordal notes above the bars.

   (b) Place an asterisk above each non-chordal note.

   (c) Explain the mistakes you find in each bar. (According to the guidelines, there is at least *one* mistake per bar.)

2. Write melodies to the rhythmic patterns below in the required keys. Play your melodies with chordal accompaniment. *Note:* Before writing your melody you should write out the chord progression (the Roman numerals I–IV–V–I) underneath the staff and the letter names of the chord notes above the staff.

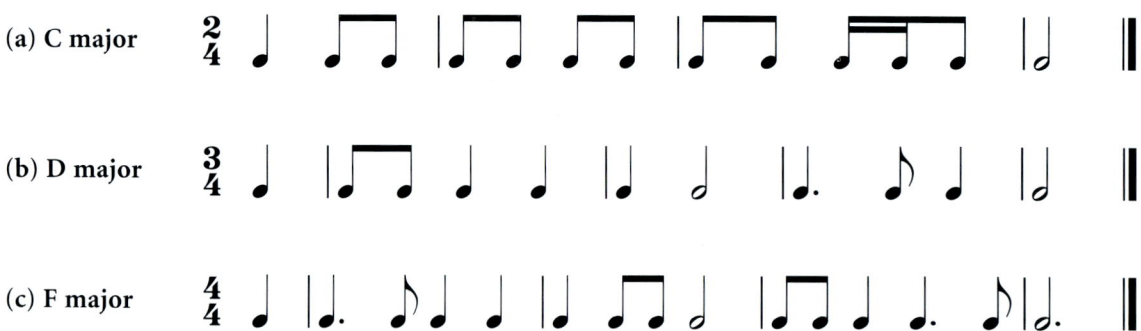

 Aural activity

Notate simple four-bar melodies played to you by your teacher.

SYMPHONY NO. 25 IN G MINOR, FIRST MOVEMENT, EXCERPT

from *AMADEUS* (WOLFGANG AMADEUS MOZART)

Tom Hulce as the giggling Mozart in Amadeus

Amadeus, the 1984 multi-award winning film adaptation of Peter Shaffer's successful play, expands on the Viennese legend concerning the death in 1791 of the musical genius W.A. Mozart, one of the greatest composers of the classical period. In flashback, the aging composer Antonio Salieri (1750– 1825) recalls how his jealousy caused him to use his influence at the Austrian court to sabotage Mozart's career. This resulted in Mozart's early death in poverty and his burial in a pauper's grave. The film uses Mozart's music exclusively throughout, the pieces being chosen by director Milos Forman and

conductor Sir Neville Marriner to underscore the
moods of the various scenes.

The first piece to be heard is an excerpt from the first
movement of the Symphony No. 25 in G minor. (A **symphony** is a large instrumental work for orchestra, which
usually has four movements.) This symphony, written in
1773 when Mozart was just 17, is scored for two oboes, two
bassoons, two horns in B flat, two horns in G, first and
second violins, violas, cellos and double basses—a standard-
size eighteenth century orchestra.

Behind the opening credits the story begins to unfold.
Salieri is hidden by a closed door but his voice is heard
crying, 'Forgive me Mozart!'. The two servants waiting
outside with his meal hear moaning and a muffled crash.
As they burst through the door the symphony begins. It
immediately establishes an agitated, dramatic mood with a
syncopated, downward-leaping four-bar theme on strings.
The minor key, based on the minor scale (see page 84),
provides a dark, sombre tonal colour.

F. Murray Abraham's chilling
portrayal of the vengeful Saller!
won him an Oscar for Best Actor.
Other awards won by *Amadeus*
included Best Director, Best
Adaptation of Material Based on
Another Medium, Best Costumes
and Best Make-Up. Academy
Awards were also received for
Sound and Art Direction.

Salieri, knife in hand and covered with blood from his
bleeding throat, looks at the servants, tries to speak and falls
backwards. To the accompaniment of ascending triadic
quavers and bustling semiquaver runs commencing at bar 5,
the servants rush to load Salieri onto a stretcher pulled by a
horse and hurry off through the snow into the night.

At bar 13, the oboes take over the melody, their mournful
tones seeming to bewail Salieri's sad fate as the music becomes gradually softer. A three-beat silence at bar 28 is a
signpost for a new theme and a different scene. The major
key theme with an octave leap upwards and demisemiquaver
ornamentation transports us to a happier occasion in a grand
Viennese ballroom.

THE BASIC PLOT of *Amadeus*

The film begins in the 1820s with the suggestion that the aging composer Salieri (F. Murray Abraham) might have murdered Mozart (Tom Hulce). It shows Salieri attempting suicide and being taken to an asylum where he confesses to a young priest his obsessive hate and jealousy of Mozart's genius. In flashback he is shown constantly sabotaging the young composer's interests, keeping him from fame and fortune at the court of the Austrian Emperor Joseph II. Mozart, ill, overworked and desperate for money, accepts a commission from Salieri, mysteriously disguised as a patron, for a Requiem (a mass for the dead) which Salieri hopes to claim as his own. Believing the Requiem to be for his own death, Mozart struggles to complete it, dictating passages to Salieri. He dies before its completion and is buried in a pauper's grave.

This is the music of the late eighteenth century court. The screen images flash repeatedly from the happy ballroom scene to Salieri being rushed through the night. At bar 59 a new theme with appoggiaturas and staccato articulation is heard enhancing the urgency as the gates of the asylum open to admit the little cavalcade with its gruesome burden. (An **appoggiatura** is an ornament that takes the accent and part of the time value of the main note.)

At bar 74, semiquaver scale passages and first violin *tremolos* show that all is bustle and activity, with lanterns waving and the figures disappearing through the open doorway. (A tremolo on a stringed instrument is a quivering effect produced by the rapid alternation of down bow and up bow.) The repeat sign indicates a return to the beginning, and the first 12 bars of the music are heard again before the scene changes.

Listen to the excerpt from Mozart's Symphony No. 25, following the score in the *Score Book*.

COMPOSER PROFILE

The Austrian composer Wolfgang Amadeus Mozart (1756–91) was a child prodigy, playing harpsichord, violin and organ, and by the age of six was acclaimed with enthusiastic praise in the courts of Europe when he toured with his talented elder sister and his musician father. He wrote his first compositions at the age of six, his first symphony when he was eight, and his first opera at the age of 12. Public interest waned as Mozart grew older and he was unable to obtain a position worthy of his talents. When he objected to being treated as a lowly servant by the Archbishop of Salzburg, Mozart was dismissed and went to Vienna. There he had some success with his operas *The Marriage of Figaro*, *Don Giovanni* and *The Magic Flute*. In his short life Mozart wrote more than 600 compositions, including 41 symphonies, nearly 20 operas and operettas, and more than 20 piano concertos.

Exploring Film Music

Score reading notes to Symphony No. 25

The instruments used in Mozart's Symphony No. 25 are oboes (*Oboi*), bassoons (*Fagotti*), horns in B flat and G (*Corni*), first and second violins (*Violino I and II*), violas (*Viole*), and cellos and basses (*Violoncello e Basso*). (Note: The horns are transposing instruments and play in a different key from the other instruments.) The score used for such a group is an **orchestral score**. In an orchestral score the instruments are laid out in families, with woodwind always placed at the top, followed by brass, percussion and strings. (You will notice that this score has no percussion.)

Note the following:

1. Instruments belonging to the same family have a bracket placed on the left-hand side of the staff line.
2. When two staves are used for the same instrument an additional brace joins them together, for example horns and violins.
3. Bar lines join the staves of instruments of the same family.

4. A treble clef is used for oboes, horns and violins.
5. An **alto clef**, which sets middle C on the middle line, is used for the viola.
6. A bass clef is used for bassoons, cellos and basses.
7. Cellos and basses in this score read the same music. However, the bass notes sound an octave lower than the cello notes.
8. The tempo indication (*Allegro con brio*—lively and fast with vigour) is written above the top staff in line with the time signature.
9. Dynamic markings are placed under each staff.
10. Music for horn does not usually have a key signature; instead, accidentals are written in front of notes where they are required.

 **Practical activity**

Perform the opening theme of Mozart's *Eine kleine Nachtmusik*, found on page 86.

MINOR SCALES, KEYS AND KEY SIGNATURES

One of the main factors contributing to the sorrowful and tragic mood of the opening section of *Amadeus* is the use of music written in a minor key, that is, music based on a minor scale that has an arrangement of tones and semitones different from that of a major scale. The notes played by the violins in the first eight bars of Symphony No. 25 are written below.

You will notice that the first note is G above the staff and the first note in bar 5 is G on the second line of the staff. If you look at the music of bars 1–8 you will find every note between the two Gs. Written as a scale, these notes would form the **G harmonic minor scale** (or simply the G minor scale) below.

G minor scale

84

Notice that in a minor scale semitones occur between the second and third, fifth and sixth, and seventh and eighth degrees. (These have been indicated by slurs in the scale on the previous page.) The other intervals are tones, except that between the sixth and seventh degrees, which is a tone and a half, or three semitones.

The score and the excerpt given above have a key signature of two flats, B♭ and E♭. However, you will see that the music has an added accidental, a sharp sign placed in front of every F, the leading note of the scale. This raises the note one semitone. In a minor scale the seventh degree, the leading note, is always raised one semitone by an added accidental. This accidental is never written as part of the key signature. (The raised leading note is the only point of difference between the harmonic minor scale and the natural minor scale.)

In bar 29 where the scene changes to the ballroom, the music changes to a bright major key. The second violins now play F♮ instead of F♯. The music has moved to the major key with the same key signature of two flats—B flat major. Major and minor keys that have the same key signatures are said to be related; for example, G minor is the **relative minor** of B flat major and B flat major is the **relative major** of G minor. Minor keys are three semitones lower in pitch than their relative major keys.

The key signatures of all the minor keys are given on page 144. Note that A minor is the relative of C major and therefore has no key signature.

 ## Aural activity

A number of scales will be played to you. Identify them as major, natural minor, harmonic minor, chromatic, whole tone and pentatonic.

 ## Written activities

1. Write the scales of A minor, D minor and E minor one octave ascending, using key signatures for D minor and E minor. Mark the semitones with slurs.
2. Write the scales of A minor, D minor and E minor one octave descending. Do not use a key signature, but write accidentals in front of notes that require them. Mark the semitones with slurs.

 ## Practical activities

1. Learn to play the scales of A, D and E minor ascending and descending.
2. Sing 'The Windmills of Your Mind' from *The Thomas Crown Affair,* which is given in the *Score Book.* The song begins and ends in the key of E minor.
3. Perform the minor melodies on page 87 which are taken from works by Mozart. (The first has been transposed for ease of playing.) Identify the key of each.
4. Learn to play the scales of B, F sharp, C sharp, G, C and F minor ascending and descending.

 ## Written and Practical activity

Select appropriate words (or write your own) and compose a song using a minor key. Perform your song with keyboard/guitar accompaniment.

A MOZART THEME TO PLAY

The main theme from the first movement of Mozart's *Eine kleine Nachtmusik* is one of the composer's most famous melodies. Written in 1778, *Eine kleine Nachtmusik* belongs to a group of light, tuneful works called 'serenades', 'divertimenti' and 'cassations' that were intended purely for entertainment, either indoors or outdoors. The work is one of many compositions by Mozart featured in the film *Amadeus*.

Eine kleine Nachtmusik (opening theme)

Mozart

Symphony No. 40, first movement

Mozart

Piano Concerto, K.491, third movement

Mozart

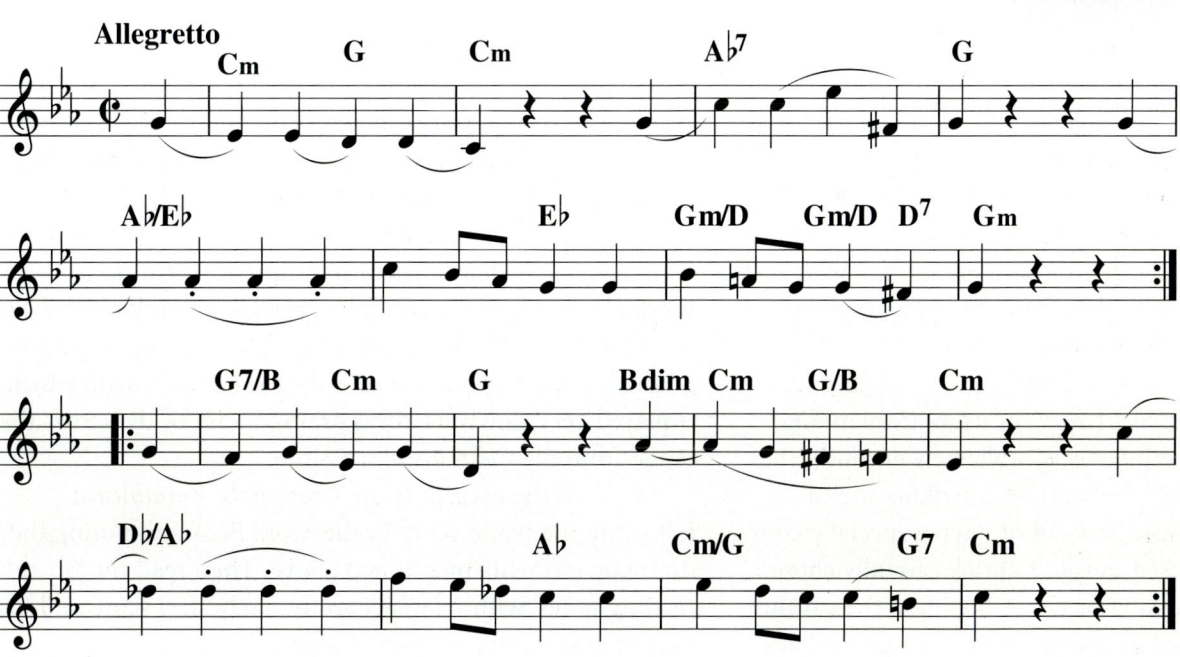

THUS SPAKE ZARATHUSTRA, EXCERPT AND REQUIEM, EXCERPT

(RICHARD STRAUSS) (GYÖRGY LIGETI)

from *2001: A SPACE ODYSSEY*

The 1968 film *2001: A Space Odyssey* is considered a milestone of the science fiction genre. Based on a short story by Arthur C. Clarke and directed by Stanley Kubrick, the film deals with the evolution of humankind from its beginnings as an ape to the human's final stage as an angelic cosmic being in a universe where time has no meaning. Space travel is seen as just one stage of this evolution or 'odyssey' to perfection, which is controlled by an extraterrestrial intelligence whose calling card is a mysterious monolith (a perfectly proportioned slab of black rock). Kubrick's thought-provoking and puzzling vision of the fate of humankind has as its central theme the struggle between humanity and machinery.

As well as being a spectacular film visually (many of its award-winning special effects broke new ground), the film also features a striking use of music. Instead of having specially composed music, Kubrick carefully chose existing pieces to highlight the various moods and ideas throughout the film.

Thus Spake Zarathustra (Richard Strauss)

Thus Spake Zarathustra, by the Austrian post-romantic composer Richard Strauss, is used at the beginning of the film under the credits and again during the 'Dawn of Man' scene to underscore the apes' dramatic discovery of the use of an object (in this case a bone) as a weapon of destruction. Kubrick selected the opening 21-bar section of this piece to create a mood of expectation and a feeling of dramatic power. The use of *Thus Spake Zarathustra* is appropriate because the opening of the work was written by Strauss to depict a sunrise. The work, written in 1896, is a **symphonic poem**, a programmatic orchestral composition with a number of descriptive sections, and is a musical statement of ideas contained in a poem by the German philosopher Friedrich Nietzsche. (The poem concerns a Persian, Zarathustra—believed to have lived in the sixth century BC—who, after spending ten years alone in the mountains, arose at dawn and addressed the sun.) *Thus Spake Zarathustra* is written for a very large orchestra with added pipe organ and creates a mood of dramatic power by use of the following elements: a soft, very low pedal note played by double basses, contra bassoon and organ pedal accompanied by a bass drum roll; a powerful three-note motive—C–G–C^1—played by trumpets to proclaim the coming sunrise; forte chords which suddenly change tonal colour from major to minor and vice versa (see page 92); forte quaver triplets on timpani and the gradual ascending pitch from bars 16–19. The piece, which is played very slowly, features dramatic use of dynamics that range from pianissimo to fortissimo.

Listen to the excerpt from *Thus Spake Zarathustra*, following the piano score in the *Score Book* and noting the dramatic elements mentioned above. Then read the 'Score reading notes' with reference to the orchestral score and listen again following the orchestral score.

THE BASIC PLOT
of *2001: A Space Odyssey*

The film begins at the 'Dawn of Man', some 4 million years ago, when plant-eating apes roamed the earth. Suddenly a strange black monolith (obviously not of this world) appears, which begins to affect the apes' behaviour. They become territorial and discover how to use bones as tools of killing. The film then jumps forward to the year 2001 AD. US scientist Dr Heywood Floyd (William Sylvester) has just boarded the rotating spaceship *Orion*, en route to the moon, where a discovery has been made in a large crater: a 4-million-year-old black monolith which emits an ear-piercing sound that seems to be directed at Jupiter. A year-and-a-half later a spaceship has been dispatched to Jupiter under the command of David Bowman (Keir Dullea) and Frank Poole (Gary Lockwood), who run the ship with the help of HAL 9000, a 'flawless' super-computer. Unfortunately HAL malfunctions and tries to take over the mission, the purpose of which only it knows. HAL kills Poole and the other three hibernating crew members but is finally outwitted and deactivated by Bowman. As the ship approaches Jupiter, Bowman learns of the lunar monolith and sees another slab passing by the spaceship. Then follows a spectacular and psychedelic sequence involving entry into another time zone, after which Bowman finds himself in an eighteenth century bedroom where he discovers an old man—himself at age 100—with whom he has an enigmatic conversation. Another monolith then appears in the room and moves towards the bed. The film concludes with an embryo (looking vaguely like Bowman) floating towards earth.

COMPOSER PROFILES

Richard Strauss (1864–1949) was the greatest German musician of the late nineteenth and early twentieth centuries. He composed his first pieces at the age of six and became a virtuoso conductor as well as a composer. His most famous works are a series of symphonic poems or tone poems and a number of operas. A post-romantic composer, he is important for his innovative use of harmony and instrumentation, and for expanding the expressive capabilities of the modern symphony orchestra.

Hungarian György Ligeti (born 1923) was a leading composer of experimental music in the 1960s. Many of his works involve the exploration of constantly changing textures and timbres. Three of Ligeti's compositions are used in *2001: A Space Odyssey*; these are Requiem for Soprano, Mezzo-Soprano, 2 Mixed Choirs and Orchestra (1965), *Lux Aeterna* for choir and orchestra (1966), and *Atmospheres* for orchestra (1961).

Score reading notes to *Thus Spake Zarathustra*

The instruments used in *Thus Spake Zarathustra* are piccolo (*Kleine Flöte—kl. Fl.*), three flutes (*Grosse Flöte—gr. Fl.*), three oboes (*Oboen*), clarinet in E flat (*Klarinette in Es*), two clarinets in B flat (*Klarinetten in B*), three bassoons (*Fagotte*), contra bassoon (*Kontrafagotte*), six horns in F (*Hörner*), four trumpets in C (*Trompete*), three trombones (*Posaune*), bass tuba (*Basstuba—Btb.*), two timpani (*Pauken*), bass drum (*Grosse Trommel*), cymbals (*Becken*), organ (*Orgel*), first and second violins (*Violinen*), violas (*Bratschen*), cellos (*Violoncelle*) and double basses (*Kontrabässe*). (Note that to conserve space on page 1, piccolo, flutes, horns 5 and 6 and bass tuba do not appear.)

As you learnt from Mozart's Symphony No. 25, woodwind instruments are placed at the top of the score with brass underneath them. Percussion instruments are always placed underneath the brass and any keyboard instrument, such as organ, is placed between percussion and strings.

Note the following:

1. First and second trombones have a tenor clef which sets middle C on the fourth line.
2. The bass drum is played with timpani sticks ('*mit Paukenschlägeln*').
3. Double basses play demisemiquaver *tremolos*, indicated by three dashes over the notes.

Requiem (György Ligeti)

György Ligeti's Requiem, written in 1965, is used to create a mystical mood and is always associated with the strange monolith, the manifestation of the extraterrestrial power guiding humankind's odyssey to the higher plane. The music is used three times in the film, firstly when the monolith appears to the apes, secondly when it is discovered on the moon and finally when it is seen flying through space as the spaceship is orbiting Jupiter. The Requiem is classified as **avant garde**, a term used to describe the works of composers of the second part of the twentieth century that feature unconventional treatment of musical elements and entirely new compositional techniques. The music is **atonal**, that is, it does not have a key. The use of this strange, unconventional music is appropriate for the mysterious extraterrestrial monolith.

Requiem was written for the following voices and instruments:

- soprano and mezzo-soprano soloists
- chorus I for 60–100 singers, dividing into 20 parts, four each of soprano, mezzo-soprano, alto, tenor and bass
- chorus II for approximately 120 singers, dividing as for chorus I
- very large orchestra, including celeste, harpsichord and harp

In his vocal works Ligeti was primarily concerned with the way the various parts combined into bands of sound or **tone clusters** of notes sung very close together that constantly change in pitch, dynamics, density and length. In Requiem Ligeti indicates that the bar lines are purely a means of organising the individual parts in time and do not mean that particular beats are to be stressed. Passages marked by a continuous black line above the music, as in the sample page of score in the *Score Book*, need be sung not in exact pitches, but as close as possible to the written notes. (That is, the mezzo-sopranos and tenors in this section sing approximate pitches.) There are few indications of breathing, every singer taking an individual breath when necessary, so that the breathing is 'staggered' to provide a smooth, continuous sound.

Listen to the excerpt of Requiem paying attention to the constantly changing musical elements.

 ## Practical activities

1. Perform the melody from Johann Strauss's *The Blue Danube* waltz on page 91.

2. Improvise, as a class or in small groups, an atonal vocal piece to create a mood or atmosphere of your choice. Your piece may contain various textures, from single sounds to tone clusters; special techniques such as glissandos; spoken and whispered sounds, shouts, and so on.

A MOVIE THEME TO PLAY

The Blue Danube waltz by the nineteenth century Austrian composer Johann Strauss (1825–99) is used in *2001: A Space Odyssey* as the spaceship approaches the Spaceport. Director Stanley Kubrick cleverly used the waltz's triple metre rhythms to suggest the huge Spaceport's slow rotating movement.

The Blue Danube waltz

Johann Strauss

MAJOR AND MINOR CHORDS

Minor intervals

In *Thus Spake Zarathustra* the mood of expectation and feeling of dramatic power are enhanced by the use of consecutive *forte* major and minor chords in bars 6–7 and minor and major chords in bars 10–11. If you look at these chords in the right-hand part of the piano score in bars 6 and 7 you will see that the notes are based on triads: CEG and CE♭ G respectively.

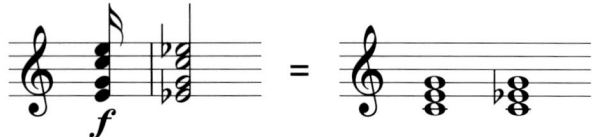

Listen as your teacher plays these triads; you will notice that they have different sound or tonal qualities. This is because the 3rd above the root of the triad is different in the second chord. In the first triad the interval from C to E is a major 3rd while in the second triad the interval between C and E♭ is a semitone smaller. This is called a minor 3rd. An interval that is a semitone smaller than a major interval is a **minor interval.**

You will remember that the major intervals in the major scale are the 2nd, 3rd, 6th and 7th. If a minor interval is a semitone less than a major interval, then only minor 2nds, 3rds, 6ths and 7ths are possible. Listen as your teacher plays the major and minor intervals below and note the differences in their quality.

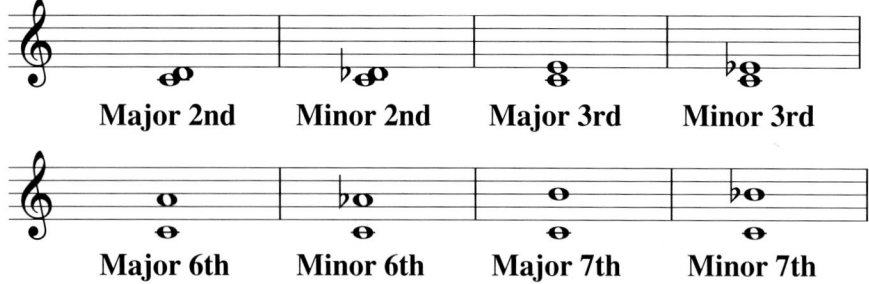

Minor intervals can be sung using solfege, as follows:

> minor 2nd—mi-fa or ti-doh[1]
> minor 3rd—mi-soh or la-doh[1]
> minor 6th—mi-doh[1] or la,-fah
> minor 7th—re-doh[1]

Note: To write a minor interval above a given note, first work out the major interval then lower the upper note one semitone. Make sure you do not alter the letter name of the upper note.

Written activities

1. Write the required minor intervals above the given notes.

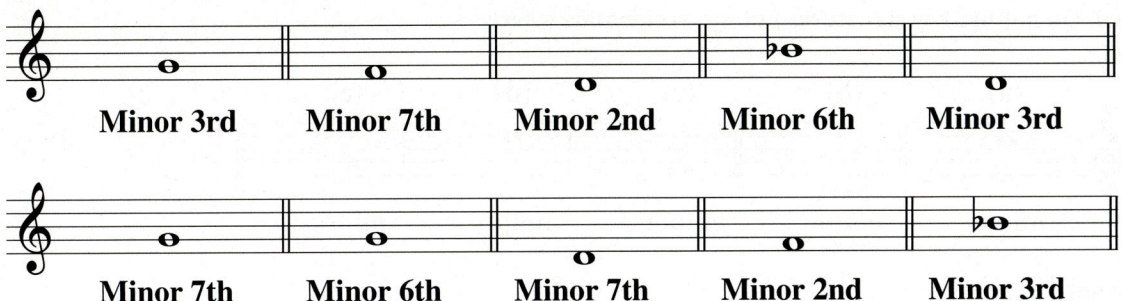

Minor 3rd   Minor 7th   Minor 2nd   Minor 6th   Minor 3rd

Minor 7th   Minor 6th   Minor 7th   Minor 2nd   Minor 3rd

2. Identify each of the following intervals according to its size and quality.

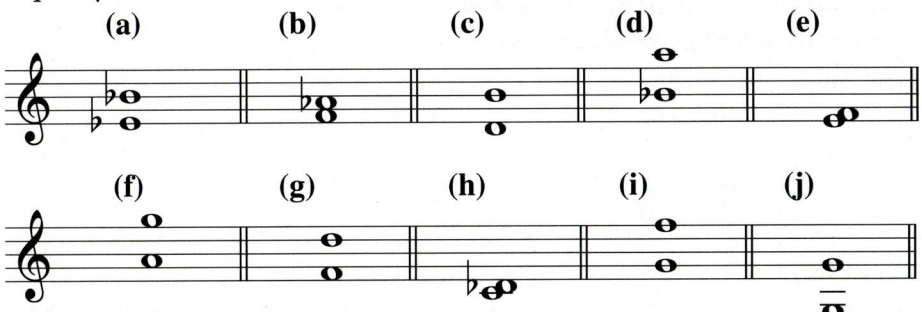

(a) (b) (c) (d) (e)

(f) (g) (h) (i) (j)

 ## Aural activity

Identify each of the major, minor and perfect intervals played to you, according to its size and quality.

Major and minor triads

Listen again as the two triads from bars 6 and 7 are played to you. The first has a bright sound and is a **major triad** because it has a major 3rd and a perfect 5th above the root. The second has a darker sound and is a **minor triad** because it has a minor 3rd and a perfect 5th above the root. Therefore we can see that it is the interval of the 3rd that determines whether a triad is major or minor.

 ## Aural activity

Listen to triads played to you by your teacher and determine whether they are major or minor.

Written activity

Write major and minor triads above the given root notes as indicated. Do not use key signatures but use accidentals where required.

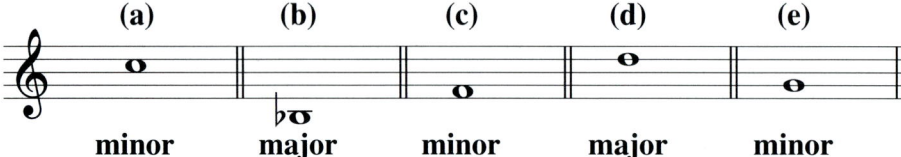

Minor chord symbols

Chord symbols written above music can indicate major or minor triads. A chord symbol consisting of a single letter, such as C, F, G or B♭, represents a major triad; to represent a minor triad the small letter 'm' is written after the chord letter, for example, Em, Gm, Dm and Am.

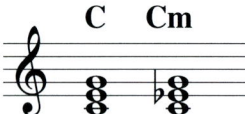

Triads in major and minor keys

In both major and minor keys some of the triads built on the scale notes are major and some are minor. From now on we will indicate major triads with large, upper case Roman numerals and minor triads with small, lower case Roman numerals. In a major key, chords I, IV and V are major and chords ii, iii and vi are minor; in a minor key, chords i and iv are minor and chords V and VI are major.

Study the triads built on the notes of the major and minor scales below. Each major or minor triad is labelled with a Roman numeral and a chord symbol. Note that in both major and minor keys certain triads do not contain a perfect 5th and thus do not qualify as either major or minor triads. These triads are indicated with an asterisk.

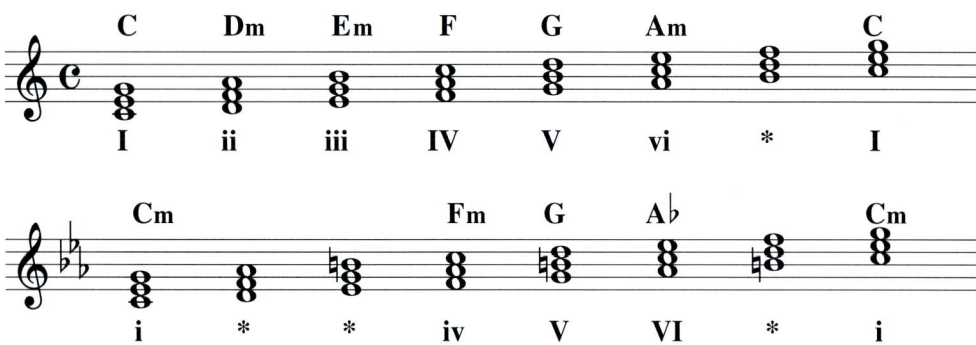

Practical activity

Sing 'The Exodus Song' from the 1960 film *Exodus* in the *Score Book*. The film, an absorbing history of the early days of the State of Israel after World War II, won an Oscar for Best Musical Score (written by Ernest Gold). The song uses the contrasting tonal colours of major and minor chords to create a dramatic effect appropriate to the subject matter.

'THIS IS A TALE'

from *BABE*

(Music by CAMILLE SAINT-SAËNS, arranged by NIGEL WESTLAKE)

The Australian movie *Babe*, awarded an Oscar for Best Visual Effects, was one of the most popular movies of 1995. Telling the tale of a piglet that wants to be a sheepdog, *Babe* captured the imagination of audiences both young and old around the world. Contributing to the fairytale quality of the film is the colourful music score by the Australian composer Nigel Westlake, who also included some arrangements of classical pieces. The main piece used is a small section from the Organ Symphony written in 1886 by the French romantic period composer Camille Saint-Saëns which is heard a number of times in different arrangements, including in the farmer's song 'If I Had Words', to provide unity.

The arrangement 'This is a Tale', is heard during the credits as portraits of pigs are shown lining the walls of a room. A short introduction—featuring silvery-toned percussion instruments such as glockenspiel, celeste (see page 97), triangle and cymbal, and other instruments including violin, fanfare-like trumpet, whistle and harp—creates a light, ethereal mood of fantasy and suggests the idea of a make-believe setting where marvellous and extraordinary events could occur. Then follows the Saint-Saëns theme given on page 97.

This is first played on celeste with responses by pizzicato (plucked) strings, light woodwind and xylophone. After a short bridging section during which the texture thickens and the volume increases, the theme is heard again *fortissimo* on full orchestra. On the final chord of the music the image changes from a portrait to a real piglet lying asleep.

Learn to play the Saint-Saëns theme before listening to the Nigel Westlake arrangement from *Babe*. Note the use of instruments to create a mood of fantasty. Then listen to an excerpt from the original organ symphony while following the score in the *Score Book*.

⚠ *Babe* **is set in a farmyard**

 Practical activity

Sing 'If I Had Words' from the *Score Book*.

THE BASIC PLOT
of *Babe*

The piglet Babe is won at a local fair by Farmer Hoggett, who takes him home in order to fatten him up for Christmas dinner. On the farm Babe soon makes some odd friends, including Ferdinand the duck who thinks he's a rooster and Fly the sheepdog whom Babe calls 'Mom'. However, Babe's approach to life is different from the rest and he refuses to accept his chosen fate. With Fly's help, and the blessing of Farmer Hoggett who senses something special in the piglet, Babe learns how to herd sheep. He is entered into the world sheepdog championship where, after a disastrous start when all the sheep simply laugh at him, he eventually triumphs.

COMPOSER PROFILE

Camille Saint-Saëns (1835–1921), organist, pianist and composer, wrote his first symphony at the age of 18 and continued composing for the next 70 years in a lyrical and elegant style. His Third Symphony in E flat minor, with organ and piano (the latter being played by four hands), is one of his greatest works. Other popular compositions include *Danse Macabre* (1874), and the suite for orchestra with two pianos, *Le carnival des animaux* (*Carnival of the Animals*) (1886).

ARRANGER PROFILE

Australian Nigel Westluke is the son of professional musicians. He studied clarinet with his father and left school early to pursue a career in music. He was soon free-lancing with many prominent orchestras and ensembles in Australia. In 1983 he furthered his studies of contemporary music in Holland, specialising in bass clarinet performance.

From 1986–1992 he was a core member of The Australian Ensemble, widely recognised as Australia's finest chamber music ensemble, touring throughout Australia and on many overseas tours to Asia, USA, Europe, the UK, New Zealand and Russia. In 1992 he joined guitarist John Williams' group 'Attacca' as a performer and composer for tours of the UK and Australia.

As a composer Westlake is largely self-taught. He was awarded an Australia Council grant to study orchestration which he completed in 1993. He has completed commissions for ensembles, orchestras, theatre, circus, television, radio and films. His film work has included several Imax (giant screen) movies and award-winning scores for *Babe*, *Children of the Revolution* and *The Edge*.

His concert work has been performed by John Williams, The London Symphony Orchestra, The Royal Scottish National Orchestra, The Australia Ensemble, Synergy Percussion, The Amsterdam Percussion Ensemble, and The Goldner String Quartet to mention but a few. He has won numerous awards including the Gold Medal at the New York Radio Festival Awards in 1988 for Best Original Music.

Organ theme from Symphony No. 3, second movement

Camille Saint-Saëns

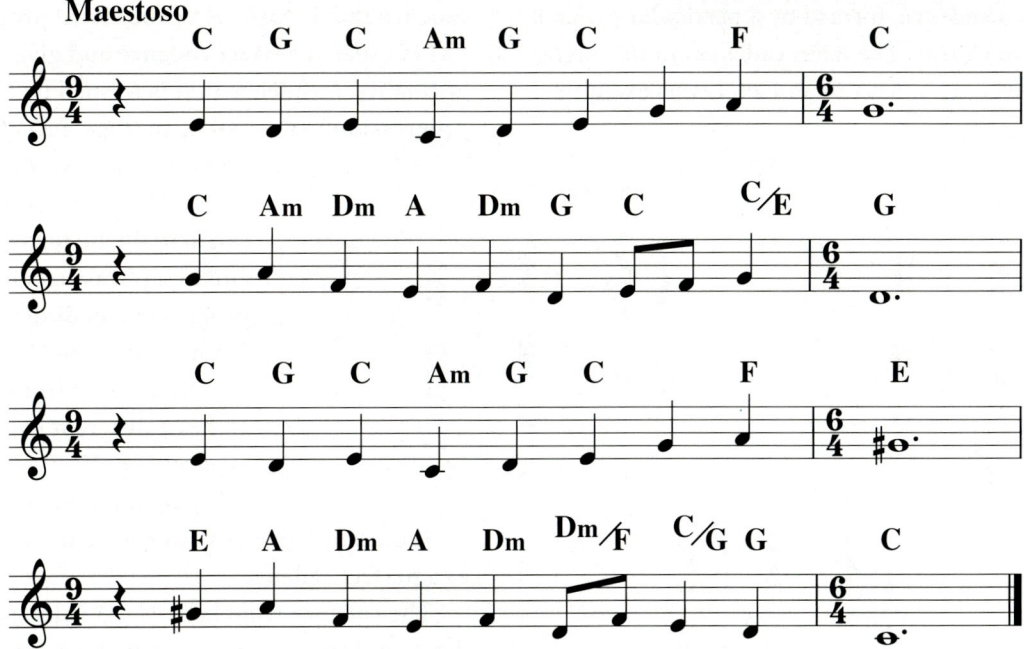

MORE COMPOUND TIME SIGNATURES

You will notice that in the excerpt from Symphony No. 3 of Saint-Säens in the *Score Book* the metre alternates between $\frac{9}{4}$ and $\frac{6}{4}$. $\frac{9}{4}$ is compound triple time with three dotted minim beats in a bar while $\frac{6}{4}$ is compound duple time with two dotted minim beats in a bar. In bar 9 of the score the violins play crotchet subdivisions of $\frac{9}{4}$, each group of three crotchet pulses being equal to a dotted minim beat.

The compound quadruple metre $\frac{12}{4}$ would have four dotted minim beats in a bar.

Note that in the piano duet parts above the strings the pianos are playing **sextuplets**, groups of six semiquavers for each crotchet pulse. A sextuplet is six notes played in the time of four of the same value.

The celeste, a keyboard glockenspiel that makes its sounds when felt-covered hammers (worked by the keys) strike metal bars. The sound is high and silvery like a music box and is ideal for creating a mood of fantasy. The classical composer Tchaikovsky used it for just such a purpose in the 'Dance of the Sugar Plum Fairy' from his Nutcracker Suite.

CADENCES

The organ music of Saint-Säens' Symphony No. 3, commencing at bar 17 in the *Score Book*, is eight bars long and comprises four two-bar phrases. At the end of each phrase the music comes to a point of rest, known as a **cadence**, formed by a particular progression of two chords. The main cadences in this eight-bar theme occur at bars 20 and 24. Let us examine these.

Study the chords used in the cadences below and listen as your teacher plays them to you. You will notice that the chord progression I–V does not seem to sound final, while V–I does. A cadence that is formed by the chord progression V–I is called a **perfect cadence** and gives a feeling of finality. A cadence that is formed by the chord progression I–V is called an **imperfect cadence** and does not give a feeling of finality. (An imperfect cadence can actually be formed at the end of a phrase by any chord progression ending with chord V, for example ii–V or IV–V.)

The cadence from bars 17–18 has a different chord progression, IV–I. Listen as this **plagal cadence** is played. It does not give as strong a feeling of finality as a perfect cadence.

The cadence from bars 21–22 belongs to a different key. To provide a new tonal colour the music has moved momentarily to A minor and this is an imperfect cadence in that key.

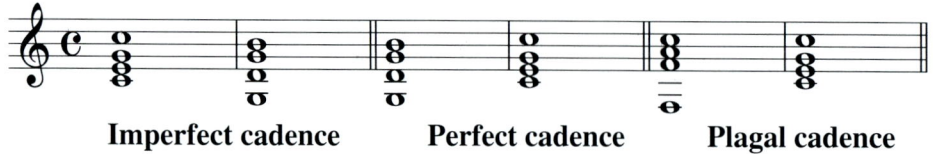

bars 19-20   bars 23-24

I   V   V   I

bars 17-18

IV   I

 Aural activity

Identify the cadences played to you by your teacher as imperfect, perfect or plagal.

 Practical activities

1. Sing the cadences given below using solfa names.

Imperfect cadence   **Perfect cadence**   **Plagal cadence**

2. Play 'Pizzicati' from *Sylvia* by Delibes on the opposite page, another classical theme used in *Babe.* The piece features many imperfect and perfect cadences.

A CLASSICAL MOVIE THEME TO PLAY

French romantic composer Léo Delibes (1836–91) wrote several operas and ballets containing much delightful and tuneful music that is still popular today. One such piece is 'Pizzicati', written for plucked strings, from the ballet *Sylvia* (1876). A variation of it is used in the scene from *Babe* where the pig enters the house to sneak past the sleeping cat and go upstairs to fetch the 'mechanical rooster'. Nigel Westlake calls his variation 'Anorexic Duck Pizzicati'. The piece contains a number of cadence points—imperfect cadences at bars 2, 6, 8 and 10, and perfect cadences at bars 4, 12 and 16. These are highlighted and made humorous in the film by dramatic pauses.

'Pizzicati' from Sylvia

Léo Delibes

Written activities

1. The music below contains three phrases. Identify the
   cadence at the end of each phrase.

2. Label each chord with a guitar chord symbol above
   and a Roman numeral below. Note that asterisks
   indicate passing notes.

'THEME FROM MISSION: IMPOSSIBLE'

from *MISSION: IMPOSSIBLE*   (LALO SCHIFRIN)

The 1996 action-thriller *Mission: Impossible* is based on the popular TV series of the same name which ran from 1966 to 1973. In each weekly episode of this series, a team of American undercover agents would carry out a risky top-secret operation, often using the latest technological devices to outwit their enemies. The film borrows elements of the series, such as having the team leader receiving his instructions through a self-destructing video-cassette (a reel of tape in the original), the high-tech gadgets and the use of the famous theme music written by Argentine composer Lalo Schifrin.

Directed by Brian De Palma, who has directed many suspense and horror films, *Mission: Impossible* is set in the world of international spies and double agents, and concerns the hero Ethan Hunt (Tom Cruise) trying to stop a Russian agent who plans to steal a computer disk in order to reveal the identities of American agents stationed in Europe. The film has several nail-biting scenes, including one in which Hunt's team of agents must break into a computer room without setting off an alarm that is sensitive to the slightest sound or movement. There is also an exciting climactic chase through the English/French Chunnel featuring a helicopter pursuing a high-speed train. Throughout the film the audience is left in the dark about what is actually happening, who the characters really are and where the story is heading as the plot twists and turns in a very complicated fashion.

Suspense is thus the pervading mood in *Mission: Impossible* and this is established at the very beginning of the film by Schifrin's brilliant theme music. The piece is a contemporary electronic arrangement of the original in G minor. It has many elements that contribute to the creation of the mood, including the opening trill, the nine bars of irregular $\frac{5}{4}$ metre (a **complex metre** made up of a combination of three beats and two beats), a syncopated two-bar bass **riff** (a repeated rhythmic melodic phrase) and disjointed melodic fragments with long notes moving in semitone steps. The famous bass riff has the following rhythmic pattern, which you should learn to clap:

Listen to the 'Theme' from *Mission: Impossible* following the Listening outline.

THE BASIC PLOT
of *Mission:Impossible*

On a self-destructing video-cassette veteran master spy Jim Phelps (Jon Voight) receives instructions directing him to carry out a mission to stop a former Russian spy revealing the identities of American espionage agents stationed in Europe. Phelps devises a master plan and assembles a team of operators, headed by his protégé Ethan Hunt (Tom Cruise), who are to steal a computer disk containing the names of the US agents. The theft is to take place at a formal embassy gala in Kiev; however in the course of the mission most of the team are liquidated. Hunt discovers that there is a 'mole' (double agent) inside the unnamed espionage bureau and, when he contacts his boss Kittridge (Henry Czerny), Hunt learns that he himself has been blamed for the killings and that he is being hunted by his own government. He then sets out to search for the real killers, and for the mysterious Bible-quoting 'Job', who is also after the disk.

Listening outline

Introduction ... Two-bar synthesised drum beat followed immediately by a long trill on the dominant that immediately establishes a mood of suspense; the trill slides upwards in a **glissando** to the tonic introducing the $\frac{5}{4}$ riff with extra electronic percussion. The riff is heard first in the bass, then harmonised with thick, savage chords.

Section A ..... Metre change to $\frac{4}{4}$; variation of the bass riff; melodic fragments with the last long notes descending by semitone step; four loud chords mark the end of the section.

Four-bar link

Section B ..... Descending low, long-note melody over a repeated one-bar bass pattern continuing for eight bars and ending with three chords

Section C ..... Ten bars of a rhythmic variation of the Section A riff in the bass followed by a further ten bars with added chords

Section A¹ .... Melodic fragments doubled at the octave

Coda .... Two bars of syncopated chords ending unexpectedly and dramatically on chord VI to heighten the feeling of suspense

 Listening activity

Notate the two-bar bass riff heard in the $\frac{5}{4}$ Introduction.

 Written and **Practical activity**

Write an eight-bar melody in a complex metre, $\frac{5}{4}$ or $\frac{7}{8}$. Perform your melody with keyboard/guitar accompaniment.

COMPOSER PROFILE

Composer, arranger and conductor Lalo Schifrin, born in Argentina in 1932, has written over 140 film and TV scores as well as numerous jazz and contemporary art-music pieces. At the start of his career in the mid 1950s he studied with the French composer Olivier Messiaen at the Paris Conservatoire while playing jazz at night-time to earn his living. Later he earned a reputation for film composing and arranging in his homeland, and in 1960 he moved to New York to become the music director of leading jazz artist Dizzy Gillespie for whom he composed many pieces. Soon he was writing for other great artists as well as pursuing a solo jazz career. In 1964 he began composing for films and television, producing memorable music for such series as *The Man From U.N.C.L.E.*, *Mannix*, *Medical Center* and *Mission: Impossible*. Films with his jazz-influenced scores include *Bullitt* (1968), *Kelly's Heroes* (1970), *Dirty Harry* (1971) and *Enter the Dragon* (1973). Turning to symphonic music (a style that became popular mainly through the efforts of John Williams) he produced a number of excellent film scores, including those for *The Four Musketeers* (1974) and *The Amityville Horror* (1979). Today Schifrin is mainly active in the classical world, conducting and recording with great international orchestras and arranging music for leading classical artists, including the 'Three Tenors'. He still produces the occasional television and film score, such as for *F/X2* (1991) and *The Beverly Hillbillies* (1993).

FILM MUSIC FOR AURAL ANALYSIS

Listen to excerpts from the 'Theme' from *Batman* and 'Parade of the Charioteers' from *Ben Hur*—two pieces of film music that create contrasting moods. The first piece is by one of today's leading young composers; the second is by one of the great composers of the so-called 'golden age' of movies, the 1930s–1950s. For each piece identify the mood of the music and point out what aspects help to create this mood. Mention such things as tonality (key), instrumental timbre, rhythm, harmony and melody. A brief background is given for each film so that you will understand the context of the music.

'Theme from *Batman*' (Danny Elfman)

from *Batman*

The 1989 film *Batman*, directed by Tim Burton, is based on the famous comic book superhero of the same name. It is set in dark and dangerous Gotham City, a place where criminals rule the streets—that is, until the appearance of the mysterious Batman (played by Michael Keaton). In his frightening, black-leather-caped, batlike disguise, the masked champion of justice—who, like a bat, appears only at night—thwarts the evil plans of the horribly disfigured Joker (played by Jack Nicholson), who has gained control of Gotham City's underworld. The opening 'Theme', by Danny Elfman, immediately suggests not only the mood of the troubled city but also the heroic qualities of its saviour.

'Parade of the Charioteers' (Miklos Rozsa)

from *Ben Hur*

Ben Hur (1959), winner of 11 Oscars (one being for Best Music Score), is one of the grandest 'epic' movies of all time. (An **epic** is a large-scale, 'blockbuster' film dealing with the adventures of an heroic individual.) Based on a novel written in 1880 by General Lew Wallace, *Ben Hur* tells the story of the Jewish prince Judah Ben Hur (played by Charlton Heston) who lives in Jerusalem in the early first century. Condemned to hard labour as a galley slave on a Roman ship for a crime he did not commit, Ben Hur swears to return and take revenge on the arresting officer Messala, his former childhood friend (played by Stephen Boyd). He eventually does this by defeating Messala in a gruelling chariot race, in a classic scene which is considered one of the most spectacular action sequences ever filmed. There is no music to the scene as the director William Wyler considered the sounds of the chariots, the thunder of the horses' hooves and the roar of the crowd to be sufficiently dramatic. However, music is used before the race begins to

herald the appearance of the brave and colourful charioteers. The magnificent 'Parade of the Charioteers' by Miklos Rozsa accompanies the men as they circle the Roman Forum in their chariots and helps create the required mood for the coming race. An important feature of the music is the use of **imitation**, the repetition of a melodic pattern by a different instrumental line or 'voice', to suggest one chariot following after another.

Activities for senior students

Composition

Imagine you are composing music to create a particular mood for a film scene. Write a short description of the scene and work out the mood or moods that would predominate. Compose an appropriate piece of music, taking into consideration such elements as timbre, texture, tonality, harmony, consonance/dissonance, melodic contour, rhythm, dynamics, and so on. You may like to include some chance elements in your composition.

Arranging

Select a piece of film music that creates a particular mood, for example 'Falls' from *The Mission*, and arrange it for available instruments, ensuring that your orchestration contributes to the creation of the mood.

Create a soundtrack

Find an appropriate piece of recorded music to create a mood for a particular film scene. Dub the music onto the film.

Research activity

Select a film in which the music creates varying moods, for example *Out of Africa* or *Dances with Wolves*, which both have music by John Barry. Select at least three different pieces used in the film and analyse the composer's use of musical elements to create the moods. You will need to quote the musical themes to which you are referring.

Oral presentation

Choose three films with scores by different composers in which the music helps to create the same mood, for example horror or suspense. Using video excerpts compare and contrast each composer's use of musical elements to create the mood.

WORDS TO KNOW

rock 'n' roll	counter melody	symphony	avant garde	plagal cadence
primary triads	ornamentation	appoggiatura	atonal	complex metre
chord progression	perfect intervals	orchestral score	tone cluster	riff
blues chord	unison	alto clef	minor interval	glissando
progression	major intervals	minor key	major triad	epic
couplet	chordal note	harmonic minor	minor triad	imitation
chorus	non-chordal note	scale	sextuplet	
chorus form	tonic	relative minor	cadence	
blue notes	leading note	relative major	perfect cadence	
harmonic rhythm	dominant	symphonic poem	imperfect cadence	

▶ Horror movies, such as the classic 1954 Creature from the Black Lagoon, rely heavily on music to express the emotions of the characters and to elicit similar responses from us

EXPRESSING EMOTIONS

Up to this point in our study of film music we have seen how composers use music to evoke a time and place, to convey character and ideas, and to create a mood or atmosphere. Let us now consider how the changing emotions of the characters, their innermost thoughts and their states of mind are communicated to the audience. In fact many people consider the primary function of any film score is to provide an emotional backdrop for the film.

The screen image can only depict the characters' outside appearances while the spoken word can tell us the emotion being experienced but cannot always adequately convey the depth of the emotion. Sometimes the characters' words and actions even mask their real feelings. It is the music that

must mirror the characters' emotional states so that
we understand exactly how they are feeling; in other
words, the music must tell us what to feel. To this end
the composer manipulates such musical elements as
tempo, timbre, pitch, tonality, rhythm, texture and
so on to match the characters' thoughts and feelings.
Thus sorrow may be represented by slow, solemn, low-
pitched music in a minor key played on brass or low
strings and woodwinds; joy by bright and light flutes,
clarinets or violins in a major key; and terror by high-
pitched string tremolos or shrill organ.

It would be impossible to examine every human
emotion in this text; let us therefore take a number
of representative emotions, including love, joy, sorrow
and terror, and see how these can be communicated
through film scores.

'NON NOBIS, DOMINE' (PATRICK DOYLE)

from *HENRY V*

🔺 *A group of English soldiers after the Battle of Agincourt from* **Henry V**

The actor and director Kenneth Branagh, born in Northern Ireland, has been responsible for a number of popular productions of Shakespeare's plays, including his 1989 film of *Henry V* which tells the story of the 1415 Battle of Agincourt in which a small English army defeated a much larger French force. The musical score was written by the Scottish composer Patrick Doyle, who has also contributed scores for Branagh's other historical films. In *Henry V* 'Non Nobis, Domine' is sung after the Battle of Agincourt. Before the battle King Henry stands upon a wagon and gives what is now known as the St Crispian's Day speech. In the film version he tells the men that, 'Yes, we might die here, or yes, we might live … but when we return home, and on this day in the years to come, men will roll up their sleeves and bare the scars and say, "Yes, I fought alongside King Henry on St Crispian's Day"'. The outnumbered English then go off to battle and defeat the French who beg to surrender in order to account for their thousands of dead. The English have lost only a small number of soldiers and three young flag-bearers. As they commence their journey back to England, King Henry says, 'Let there be sung "Te Deum" and "Non Nobis" as thanksgiving to God'.

At this point in the film the English soldiers sing the hymn of praise 'Non

Nobis, Domine', Patrick Doyle's prize-winning setting of Psalm 115, in which the emotions of love of God and country are movingly expressed. The English translation of the words, which are sung in Latin, the language of the church at the time, is 'Not to us, O Lord, not to us but to your name be the glory because of your love and faithfulness'. The composer gradually builds the emotional level by using different musical textures for each verse or repetition of the words, starting with a lone raw voice in the midst of the carnage and thickening to a massive chorus singing triumphantly. Other elements contributing to the emotional build-up include a key change and rising dynamics.

The melody for 'Non Nobis, Domine', with the Latin words, is given below. Learn to sing the song; when you are familiar with it listen to the music, following the 'Listening outline' on page 109.

> *Henry V* won an Oscar for Best Costume Design. The theme for 'Non Nobis, Domine' was voted Best Film Theme of 1989 at Britain's Ivor Novello Awards.

THE BASIC PLOT
of *Henry V*

The Shakespearean play *Henry V* concerns the final period of the Hundred Years' War between England and France when King Henry V laid claim to the French throne and to the lands won in France by his great-grandfather Edward III. When the French refused to recognise the claim, Henry invaded France with a small force and engaged in battle at Agincourt in 1415. The English were greatly outnumbered, but the obsolete tactics of the French gave them no chance against the English archers and Henry won a complete victory. His claim was acknowledged and sealed by marriage to the French princess.

COMPOSER PROFILE

Born in Scotland in 1953, Patrick Doyle began his career as an actor and composer for British television. In 1987 he joined actor/director Kenneth Branagh's Renaissance Theatre Company and wrote the music for several of Branagh's productions of Shakespearean plays, including *Hamlet, As You Like It* and *Much Ado About Nothing*. Doyle wrote his first film score in 1989 when he collaborated with Branagh on the film of Shakespeare's *Henry V*. His recent film scores include *Mary Shelley's Frankenstein* (1994), *A Little Princess* (1995) and *Sense and Sensibility* (1995).

Non Nobis, Domine

Patrick Doyle

Non no - bis Dom - in - e Dom - in - e Non no - bis Dom - in - e Sed dom - in - e Sed dom - in - e tu huc a Glor - i - a.

Note: Some syllables are sung to more than one note, indicated in the music by slurs. This word-setting device is called **a melisma**.

Listening outline

Verse 1 .... Melody sung by unaccompanied solo singer
(other sounds are heard in the background)

Verse 2 .... Melody sung by men in unison

Verse 3 .... Melody sung in unison with instrumental
counter melody

Verse 4 .... Main melody plus prominent male counter
melody and a different counter melody softly
on instruments

Verse 5 .... Change of key to a tone higher accentuates the
build-up of emotion. Main melody in unison
for four bars then the voices divide and a
lower harmony part is added

Verse 6 .... Main melody in unison with a high trumpet
playing the counter melody from 4

Instrumental
interlude .... Full orchestra

Verse 7 .... Four-part vocal harmony with instrumental
accompaniment provides a stirring climax

MUSICAL TEXTURES

Texture in music refers to the arrangement of melodic lines. In
'Non Nobis, Domine' three different types of musical texture
are used. The first, in verses 1 and 2, is **monophonic texture**—
one line of music heard by itself; verses 3, 4 and 6 have
polyphonic texture—two or more melodic lines moving
independently but heard together; verses 5 and 7 have
homophonic texture—a melodic line heard against a chordal
accompaniment.

Listen again to 'Non Nobis, Domine' noting these different
textures.

 ## Practical activities

1. Sing 'The Agincourt Carol' in the *Score Book*. The fifteenth
   century song celebrates Henry V's victory over the French.
2. Perform 'Saltarello', the fifteenth century dance melody
   given on page 110. Accompany it with a steady beat on
   hand drum. As there is only one melody line, this is an
   example of monophonic texture.
3. Sing 'The Kangaroo' in the *Score Book*: first unaccompanied
   in unison to demonstrate monophonic texture; then as a
   four-part round for polyphonic texture; then in unison
   with chordal accompaniment for homophonic texture.

Saltarello

Anonymous

Brightly

 Aural activity

Listen to pieces of music played to you by your teacher and determine their textures.

 Written activities

1. Write a counter melody to an eight- or 16-bar melody that may be either original or already written. Your counter melody should be based on the chord progression of the main melody but should be independent, with a different contour and rhythm. Perform your polyphonic composition with a classmate.
2. Write a chordal accompaniment and bass line to the melody you used in activity no. 1. (You may also like to add percussion parts.) Perform your homophonic composition with some classmates.

'THE FIGHTING DONELLYS' AND 'LEAVING HOME' (JOHN WILLIAMS)

from *FAR AND AWAY*

The 1992 film *Far and Away* is a colourful adventure dealing with Irish emigration to America in the late nineteenth century. It tells the story of Joseph Donelly, the destitute son of a poor Galway peasant, who decides to escape the tyranny of the rich English landlords and make his fortune in America, where, he is told, land is being given away free of charge. The main theme of the film is expressed at the start when Joseph's dying father tells him, 'Land is the soul of a man'. The wonderful musical score by John Williams effectively reinforces the various land-related emotions that are explored in the film: Joseph's love of his Irish homeland, his sadness at having to leave it, his yearning for his own land, and the excitement when he competes for a plot of land in Oklahoma.

For 'The Fighting Donellys', heard at the start of the film when Joseph engages in a vigorous fight with his two brothers, John Williams wrote music in the style of two lively Irish folk dances—a **jig,** in compound duple time, and a **reel**, in cut common time. The music is played by the popular Irish group The Chieftains on traditional instruments such as the tin whistle, the Celtic harp, the *bodhrán* (a goatskin covered hand drum, pronounced BOUGH-rawn) and the bones (short wooden rhythm sticks). The folklike music not only suggests the time and place but also expresses the exuberant emotions of the characters—especially Joseph, who is a talented fighter—

and their love of Ireland. The jig comprises four different sections, some of which are repeated, and the reel is in ternary form.

Listen to 'The Fighting Donellys' following the score of the melodies in the *Score Book*; then listen again, following the 'Listening outline' on the next page.

▼ *Tom Cruise as the bare-knuckle boxer Joseph Donelly engages in a gruelling fight in* **Far and Away**

THE BASIC PLOT
of *Far and Away*

It is 1892 and Ireland is ruled by ruthless English landlords. Joseph Donelly (Tom Cruise), the son of a poor Irish tenant farmer whose house is burnt down because the rent cannot be paid, swears murderous revenge on his merciless landlord. He makes his way to the landlord's mansion and when he is discovered in the stable fires his gun, only to be knocked unconscious. He is then taken into the house for treatment and subsequently becomes attracted to the landlord's headstrong and rebellious daughter Shannon (Nicole Kidman), who is tired of her dull, pampered life in which even her fiance (the evil overseer who had torched the Donelly home) has been chosen for her. Shannon yearns to go to America where she has learnt that land is being given away for free. She convinces Joseph to flee with her and the two sail off, masquerading as brother and sister. Landing in Boston they find lodgings, then employment as chicken-pluckers. Joseph's fighting talents, however, soon lead him into employment as a bare-knuckle boxer and for a while he enjoys money and fame. A series of unfortunate events leads him to abandon this life, and he leaves Shannon (whom he now discovers he loves) as he makes for Oklahoma Territory to try his luck in the land rush. Meanwhile Shannon's parents and their overseer emigrate to America, and, after finding Shannon, the four also head for Oklahoma. In a final spectacular scene involving hundreds of horseriders, wagons and runners racing across-country to find a desirable homesite, Joseph escapes death when his horse falls on him and narrowly beats Shannon's fiance to claim an attractive plot of land by a river. He now not only has his sense of identity—his soul—he also gains Shannon who at last realises where her true affections lie.

Listening outline to 'The Fighting Donellys'

JIG

Introduction **Played on bodhrán**

A .... In monophonic texture with fiddle and tin whistle in unison accompanied by bodhrán

A

B .... Melody over a drone bass consisting of a perfect 5th played on Celtic harp with bodhrán and bones on beat 2

B

C .... Melody accompanied by harp chords and rhythmic pattern on bones

A .... As before but with harp quaver patterns

D .... Melody with harp chords and bodhrán

B

Coda .... Based on B

REEL

Introduction **Played on bodhrán**

A .... Five-bar melody accompanied by harp, bodhrán and bones

B .... Four-bar melody

A¹

Coda

The music of 'Leaving Home' represents two contrasting emotions: Joseph's sadness at having to leave home, and his great love for the land he and his father and the generations before them have farmed. The composer therefore uses different themes for these emotions. The first theme is a simple, plaintive ternary-form melody played by the husky-toned panpipes with bleak, sparse accompaniment. The use of the ancient **Dorian mode** based on G (see below) reinforces the feeling of sorrow as does the smooth contour of the two-bar phrases which rises and falls mainly by step.

The second theme, with swelling legato phrases on strings, reflects Joseph's intense love for the land he regards as his own in Ireland. The emotional outpouring from the depths of his soul is reflected by the change to D major, the angular contour with octave leaps, the crescendos and diminuendos and by the freely changing metres.

Listen to 'Leaving Home' following the melody in the *Score Book*; then listen again, following the 'Listening outline' below.

Dorian mode   Dorian mode based on G

Listening outline to 'Leaving Home'

Introduction .. Pedal note with low, synthesised repeated brass motives creating a dark mood

A .... Modal melody on panpipes with low, synthesised note on beat 2 of bars 2 and 4

A

B .... Panpipes joined by flute with string and harp accompaniment

A¹ .... Panpipes with string accompaniment

C .... Ten-bar D major melody on strings, with orchestral accompaniment joined by flute for the last phrase

 ## Practical activities

1. Improvise rhythmic patterns on suitable untuned percussion instruments to accompany 'The Fighting Donellys'.

2. Play the traditional Irish melodies on pages 115–16. Note that 'The Road to Lisdoonvarna' uses the notes of the Dorian mode based on E.

Accompany the melodies with improvised rhythmic patterns on untuned percussion instruments.

3. Play 'Tara's Theme' from *Gone With the Wind* on page 117.

 ## Written activity

Write an eight-bar melody in compound duple metre using the Dorian mode based on D. For a satisfactory sound you should end the first phrase on the dominant note (A).

TRADITIONAL IRISH MUSIC

The traditional music of Ireland is one of the most prolific and vibrant types of folk music. In Ireland, and indeed any English-speaking country around the world, you are likely to find many groups dedicated to preserving the rich musical heritage of the Celtic race who have inhabited Ireland for thousands of years. Irish music is not static or unchanging, or even restricted to traditional-style groups; many modern Irish composers, such as Van Morrison, and Bill Whelan, the composer of the popular Irish music and dance spectacular *Riverdance*, have written songs in a traditional style. Pop groups such as Clannad, The Pogues and The Corrs have also combined elements of Irish music with contemporary rock to produce a unique 'Celtic-rock' style.

Traditional Irish music is predominantly of rural origin, and is usually performed for recreation and not for payment. Solo performance, in which subtleties of expression can best be heard, is at the heart of the tradition, but group performance in pubs, clubs and so on is common. The music is essentially monophonic; singing is normally in unison. Instruments are also played in unison in combinations of any number. Harmonic accompaniment, when possible on an instrument, is generally simple in nature. Musical forms used in songs and instrumental pieces are typically small-scale structures, such as binary or ternary forms, in which variations of text, rhythm, phrasing and melody, but rarely of dynamics, are employed. Songs are performed in both Irish and English, but those in English (the more recent) are more common. Irish melodies generally have key signatures of one or two sharps and are based on a number of seven-note modes, though five- and six-note modes are also used.

Most instrumental music is fast regular dance music—jigs, reels and **hornpipes**—while slower pieces are usually especially composed for a particular instrument or adapted from a song melody. String, wind and reed melody instruments predominate, especially fiddle (violin), Celtic harp, tin whistle, wooden flute, *uilleann* (pronounced ILL-en) pipes, concertina and accordian; percussion instruments, such as the bodhrán (a small hand drum) and bones (rhythm sticks) also play an important part. The timbres of the wind instruments (tin whistle, flute and uilleann pipes) are considered to be at the heart of the music, and it is these timbres that give Irish music its unique, haunting quality.

RESTS IN COMPOUND TIME

In compound time a one-beat silence may be indicated by:

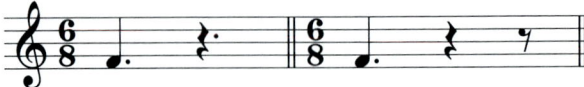

As in (b) above a crotchet rest may be used for the first and second pulses of a beat, but it must never be used for the second and third pulses. Each of these must be indicated by separate rests (as in bars 2, 6 and 12 of 'The Road to Lisdoonvarna' on page 115). Study the correct and incorrect examples below.

Correct   Incorrect

As in simple time a whole bar of silence is indicated by a semibreve rest.

 Written activities

1. Write these time signatures:
   (a) compound triple (b) compound duple
   (c) compound quadruple
2. Describe these time signatures:
   (a) $\frac{12}{8}$ (b) $\frac{9}{8}$ (c) $\frac{6}{8}$

3. Fill each bar with quavers correctly grouped.

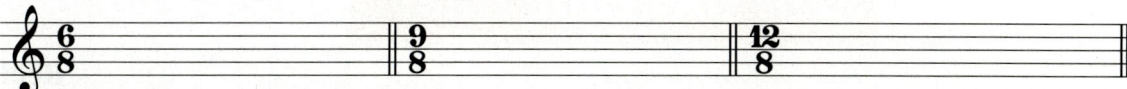

4. Complete each bar by adding rests.

5. Set the couplets below to four-bar rhythmic patterns in $\frac{6}{8}$ time.

(a) See-saw, Margery Daw,
  Jenny shall have a new master.

(b) Little Jack Horner sat in a corner,
  Eating his Christmas pie.

(c) Old Mother Hubbard went to the cupboard
  To fetch her poor dog a bone.

(d) To market, to market, to buy a fat pig,
  Home again, home again, jiggety-jig.

6. Set the following words to an eight-bar melody in $\frac{6}{8}$ time.
O! Ladies and gentlemen, please draw near;
I'll sing of a squire who lived in County Clare.
A fine young fellow he had for his man
To do his business, his name was called Dan.

 Aural activity

Notate the compound duple rhythmic patterns
played to you by your teacher.

The Road to Lisdoonvarna

Jig

The Glenmore Hunt

Reel

Off to California

Hornpipe

AN EMOTIONAL THEME TO PLAY

The 1939 film *Gone With the Wind* won eight Academy Awards and is considered by many to be the greatest movie ever made. Set during the turbulent American Civil War (1861–65), the film follows the changing fortunes of Scarlett O'Hara, fiery daughter of an Irish immigrant who builds a mansion called Tara on a cotton plantation near Atlanta. Scarlett is dispossessed of the house and land by the war and her yearning to return is expressed by the famous 'Tara's Theme', a constant feature of which is the upward octave leap that helps to express the idea of yearning.

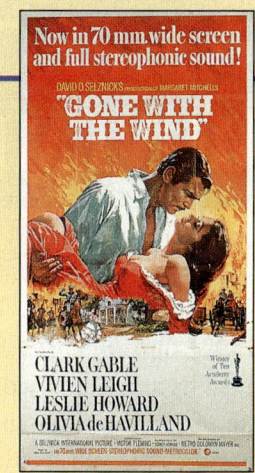

'Tara's Theme' *from* Gone with the Wind

Max Steiner

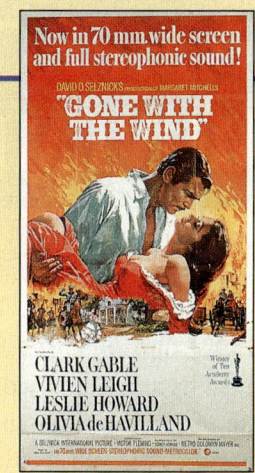

SYMPHONY NO. 9, FOURTH MOVEMENT, EXCERPT

from *IMMORTAL BELOVED*   (LUDWIG VAN BEETHOVEN)

The 1994 film *Immortal Beloved*, like *Amadeus*, is a fictionalised account of the life of a composer—in this case, the German Ludwig van Beethoven (1770–1827). Based on a script by its director Bernard Rose, the film explores the romantic mystery surrounding the unknown lady Beethoven secretly adored, his 'Immortal Beloved', who supposedly inspired him to write his monumental works. Bernard Rose takes an unusual approach in his storytelling. Using a number of Beethoven's most important and popular compositions, including piano solos, works for small ensembles and symphonies, he lets the music suggest the images and content of the scenes. In the director's own words, 'This music is a record of Ludwig van Beethoven's passions, fears, anger, and, finally, victory over adversity. It is astonishing, the strength and depth of emotion that Beethoven unleashes on the listener'. Rose continues, 'We made *Immortal Beloved* because of this music and for no other reason. The film was written, shot and edited to the score'. *Immortal Beloved* is thus an extraordinary film about an extraordinary composer—a film in which the music becomes the mouthpiece of its main character, expressing his volatile personality through a vast range of emotions, from the depths of despair to sublime joy.

An important aim of the director was to show Beethoven as a link between music of the eighteenth century—the so-called classical period in which balance and order were paramount—and music of the nineteenth century—the romantic period which stressed emotion and individualism. Rose depicts Beethoven both as a Casanova seeking ideal love and as a romantic yearning to express himself creatively through music. (The composer once said, 'I must write for what weighs on my heart, I must express'.) Expressiveness, or emotion, can clearly be heard through the film's use of popular classics such as the piano solos 'Für Elise' and the *Moonlight* Sonata, and orchestral works like the Fifth and Ninth Symphonies.

Beethoven's Ninth Symphony is sometimes called the *Choral* Symphony because of the inclusion of soprano, alto, tenor and baritone soloists and a four-part choir who sing 'Song of Joy' with words by the German poet Schiller. Play the famous melody shown on the opposite page.

The *Choral* Symphony excerpt from the fourth movement occurs towards the end of the film, the flashback showing the beautifully staged premiere. As the 'Song of Joy' fills the concert hall, the completely deaf composer steps onto the stage, hearing the music only in his head. Silence falls as Beethoven stands there and this time we hear what he hears—just the beating of his heart. This merges into a drum beat that introduces the section of the movement marked *Alla marcia* (like a march) in fast compound duple time in B flat major.

Song of Joy

Ludwig van Beethoven

The film flashes further back as the music reminds Beethoven of his difficult childhood with his brutal father. We see the young Beethoven gazing with yearning at the star-studded heavens to a rhythmic variation of the 'Song of Joy' on woodwinds and horns. This immediately suggests that through this sublime music Beethoven can escape from harsh reality. As his father arrives home the tenor soloist is heard and is joined by the tenors and basses of the chorus, the woodwinds and horns continuing their variation. To escape his father the young boy flees through the woods, his despair and agitation apparent in the music from bar 101 with fast quavers, many repeated notes, fortissimo dynamics, syncopated sforzandos, rising sequences (for example violin I bars 121–132, and bassoons, violas, cellos and basses bars 141–146), chromaticism and changing tonality to end in B minor at bar 172. The boy reaches the sanctuary of the moonlit lake and begins to take off his shirt as the orchestra breaks into a dramatic, fortissimo, syncopated unison F sharp, the dominant of B minor at bar 187, a Beethoven signpost that something important is about to happen and that a new musical idea is imminent.

At bar 195, the horns alone, gradually becoming softer, continue with an F sharp pedal note. As the boy enters the water and lies down, a three-note motive heard three times echoes the opening of 'Song of Joy', introducing a final triumphant climax in D major from chorus and full orchestra, and we see the most stunningly beautiful scene of the film: the camera pulls away as the boy floats and is emotionally transported, lost in an oblivion of stars. The section ends as Beethoven, recalled to his surroundings, is made aware of the tumultuous standing ovation from the audience and acknowledges it with joy and wonderment.

Listen to the excerpt from the Ninth Symphony, following the score in the *Score Book*. Then read the 'Score reading notes' on page 121 and listen again to the music.

THE BASIC PLOT
of *Immortal Beloved*

Shortly after the death of Ludwig van Beethoven (Gary Oldman), a letter is found among his papers: 'All my music and all the capital of my estate shall go to my sole heir … my Immortal Beloved'. This mystery woman, the one who inspired Beethoven to create his master-pieces, then becomes the object of an intense search by the composer's loyal secretary Anton Schindler (Jeroen Krabbé). Through a series of flashbacks we also see other aspects of the composer's stormy life, including childhood abuse by his father and Beethoven's dreadful treatment of his sister-in-law. (When his brother Casper dies, Beethoven uses his influence with the nobility to have her declared unfit to be the mother of his nephew Karl. He then tries unsuccessfully and with disastrous results to make Karl a genius composer and performer like himself.) We learn of his progressive hearing loss and of its painful and isolating consequences. The film paints the picture of Beethoven as a man who could not experience the beauty he created and who found in his frustration the fuel of his rage.

Who was Beethoven's 'Immortal Beloved'? Was it one of the countesses who loved him— Johanna Reiss, Anna Marie Erdody or Giulietta Guicciardi—or was it his sister-in-law?

COMPOSER PROFILE

Ludwig van Beethoven was born at Bonn in 1770 into a poor but musical family. His father was his first music teacher and believed his son to be a second Mozart. Accordingly he forced him to practise many hours every day, neglecting his other education and constantly maltreating him. The young Beethoven felt isolated, and suffered because of the degradation brought on his family by his drunken father. His music was his only solace and relief. Beethoven settled in Vienna in 1792 and quickly became famous as a pianist, much in demand at concerts. It was not until 1800 that he began to be regarded as a composer of note. Beethoven was the first composer who was able to live without the patronage of a member of the nobility, but he was dependent on influential and wealthy supporters for commissions and concerts. The first signs of his deafness appeared about 1800 and he despaired about the life of isolation ahead of him. The deafness progressed until the loss of hearing was total by about 1814 and he could no longer appear as a concert soloist. However, his musical output continued unabated until his death in 1827. Beethoven was a perfectionist, composing slowly and metic-ulously with constant revision. His compositions include nine symphonies, 32 piano sonatas, 17 string quartets, eight concertos, an opera, a mass, and many smaller works. His music is dramatic and often stormy, the result of the troubled personality he developed because of the many unhappy experiences in his life. One of music's greatest innovators, Beethoven is regarded as the last great classical composer and the first romantic.

 ## Practical activities

1. Perform the Beethoven melodies on pages 121–2.
2. Perform Minuet in G by Beethoven from the *Score Book.*

Score reading notes to Symphony No. 9

The instruments used in this section of the fourth movement are: piccolo, two flutes, two oboes, two clarinets in B flat, two bassoons, contra bassoon, two horns in D, two horns in B flat, two trumpets in B flat, timpani, triangle, cymbals, bass drum, violins I and II, violas, cellos and double basses. This was the first time triangle, cymbals and bass drum were used in a symphony.

Note the following:

1. Clarinets, horns and trumpets do not have key signatures because they are **transposing instruments** and their music in this section is in the key of C major (see page 123).
2. The word 'tacet' written beside trumpet I means that it will be silent while trumpet II plays alone.
3. At bar 103 the score indicates the use of trumpets in D. These enter at bar 213. They are smaller trumpets and have a brighter, more penetrating timbre.
4. The untuned percussion is placed beneath the timpani and written on single lines instead of staves.
5. The vocal lines are written above the strings. Note that the tenor lines are written in treble clef, an octave higher than they sound, to avoid too many ledger lines.
6. The chorus, when it enters at bar 213, comprises sopranos, altos, tenors and basses.

Sonatina for Piano in G Major (Romance)

Beethoven

Sonata for Piano, Op. 49, No. 2

Beethoven

Theme from the fifth movement of Symphony No. 6 *(Pastorale)*

Beethoven

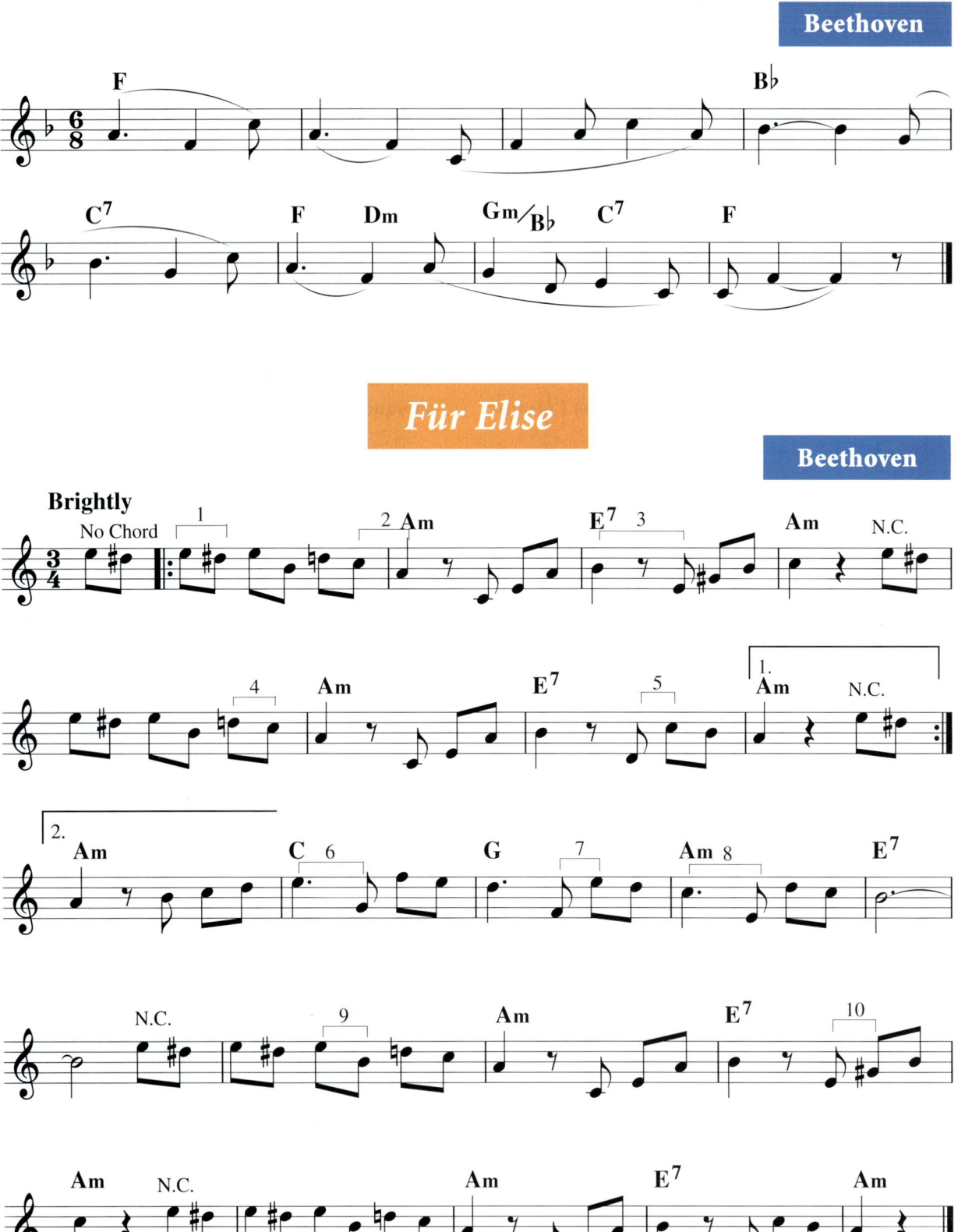

Für Elise

Beethoven

Score reading activity

Study the music of 'Für Elise' (opposite) and do the following:

1. Name the key and give three reasons for your answer.
2. Name the key to which the music modulates in the third line. State how you know it is no longer in the original key.
3. Give the name used to describe the relationship of the second key to the first.
4. Determine the range of the melody.
5. Use one word to describe the contour of the melody in the third line, for example, smooth, angular.
6. Locate and identify with bar numbers a three-bar sequence.
7. Use one word to describe the note D sharp each time it occurs.
8. State the type of chord indicated by the chord symbol 'Am'.
9. State the type of chord indicated by the chord symbol 'E7'.
10. There are ten intervals marked on the music with brackets. Identify them according to their size and quality.

TRANSPOSING INSTRUMENTS

If you study the first page of the excerpt from Beethoven's Ninth Symphony, fourth movement, you will notice that all woodwind instruments except clarinets have the key signature of B flat major. As already stated, clarinets are transposing instruments and their part is written in a key different from that of the non-transposing instruments. This movement uses clarinets in B flat (they are called 'Clarinetti in B' because B signifies B flat in many European countries). This means that when the clarinettist plays C we hear the note a tone lower, B flat, the key of the instrument. Therefore, if we wish to hear a clarinet part sound in B flat major, it must be written a tone higher in C major. To illustrate this the flute and first clarinet parts from bar 13 to bar 17 are given below. The instruments are actually playing in unison.

By looking at the score you will notice that other instruments are also transposing: horns I and II are in D and so when they play C we hear D above, the key of the instrument; horns III and IV and trumpets are in B flat like the clarinets and when they play C we hear B flat.

Written activities

1. The following melodies are written for oboe. Rewrite them
    for a clarinet so that they will sound at the same pitch.
    (Remember to use the key signature for the new key.)
    Note: If the oboe part contains an accidental you will need
    to add an accidental to the clarinet part to make the note
    one tone higher than the oboe note.

(a)

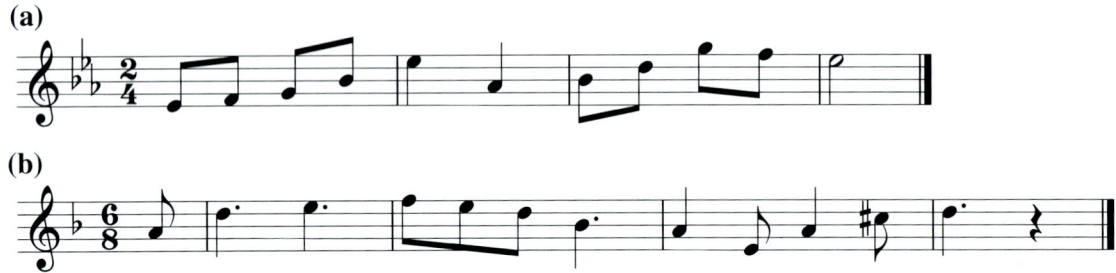

(b)

2. The following melodies are written for clarinet. Rewrite
    them for a violin so that they will sound at the same pitch.

(a)

(b)

3. Arrange the piano score of Beethoven's 'Minuet in G' given
    in the *Score Book* (or a score of your own choice) for your
    class to play. Make sure that parts for transposing
    instruments are in the correct keys and are written at the
    correct pitch. A chart showing practical instrumental
    ranges and transpositions is given on page 147.

EIGHT- AND 16-BAR MELODY WRITING

The 'Song of Joy' melody on page 119 is made up of 4 four-bar phrases: the first, second and fourth are similar, while the third is contrasting. This produces a ternary form melody with an AA¹BA¹ phrase structure which is one of the most frequently used song forms. Notice the cadences used at the ends of the phrases. The A phrase ends with an imperfect cadence; the A^1 phrases end with a perfect cadence; and the B phrase, which ends on beat 3 of bar 12, also has an imperfect cadence.

If you study the structure of the 'Sonatina' theme on page 121 you will notice that it has 2 four-bar phrases, giving a binary form AB phrase structure, the A phrase ending with an imperfect cadence and the B phrase ending with a perfect cadence.

The melodic form you use in song writing often depends on the structure and length of the lyrics.

To write a simple eight-bar melody you may like to use the following chord progression:

```
I  |  IV  |  I  |  V  |
I  |  ii  |  V  |  I  || 
```

To write a simple 16-bar melody the chord progression at right may be used. (In this progression the first, second and fourth phrases are identical and end with a perfect cadence.)

```
I  |  IV  |  V  |  I  |
I  |  IV  |  V  |  I  |
V  |  I   |  ii |  V  |
I  |  IV  |  V  |  I  ||
```

Once you have mastered writing simple eight- and 16-bar melodies to the suggested chord progressions you should work out more interesting progressions that include two or more chords per bar and that use the minor chords ii and vi to add contrasting tonal colours. Also write 16-bar melodies that end the first phrase on chord V, as in the Beethoven 'Song of Joy'.

Written activities

1. Write an eight-bar melody in the key of F major to the following rhythmic pattern:

2. Write an eight-bar melody to the following words from the poem 'Summer Evening' by Walter de la Mare:

   In the dewy fields the cattle lie
   Chewing the cud 'neath a fading sky;
   Dobbin at manger pulls his hay:
   Gone is another summer's day.

3. Write a 16-bar melody in the key of G major to the following rhythmic pattern:

4. **Write a 16-bar melody to the following words from A. E. Housman's poem 'When I was One-and-Twenty':**

   When I was one-and-twenty,
   I heard a wise man say,
   'Give crowns and pounds and guineas
   But not your heart away;
   Give pearls away and rubies,
   But keep your fancy free.'
   But I was one-and-twenty,
   No use to talk to me.

5. Write a 16-bar melody for a solo instrument with piano accompaniment. The instrument should be one available in your class. Use correct transposition if it is a transposing instrument. You may like to add a two- or four-bar introduction for the piano. Include phrasing, dynamics and any other expression terms and signs you consider appropriate for performance.

 Practical activity

Sing 'The Rose' in the *Score Book*. The song, from the 1979 film of the same name, uses rhyming couplets throughout and has an AABA[1] phrase structure.

Analytical activity

Analyse melodies for their phrase structures, including those on pages 115–16 and 121–2.

'PRELUDE' AND 'THE MURDER'

from *PSYCHO*   (BERNARD HERRMANN)

◀ *Anthony Perkins as Norman Bates talking to Janet Leigh as Marion Crane in the horror classic* Psycho

Alfred Hitchcock's *Psycho* holds a special place in the history of the horror movie. When it was released in 1960, *Psycho* created unbelievable public hysteria and broke all previous box-office records. With its treatment of such taboos as nudity, bloody murders, transvestism, voyeurism and schizo-phrenia, *Psycho* shocked audiences who had never seen anything like it before.

The film, essentially a murder mystery, concerns the stabbing of a young woman, Marion Crane, in an isolated motel run by a deranged young man named Norman Bates. Marion has stolen a large sum of money and is on the way to Fairville, California to begin a new life with her lover Sam Loomis. From the moment Marion begins her drive, Hitchcock—in typical fashion—relentlessly builds the tension, adding shock after gruesome shock until the very last scene.

A large part of the dramatic tension created in *Psycho* is due to the brilliant and chilling score by Bernard Herrmann, considered by many to be the greatest film music composer of all time. Herrmann, who worked with Hitchcock on several films, used only strings for the legendary *Psycho* music, 'to complement the black-and-white photography of the film with a black-and-white score'. The use of strings, however, did not limit the tonal colours available to Herrmann. He was a brilliant orchestrator and used such string effects as glissandos, pizzicatos, tremolos, mutes, extremes of registers, harmonics, bowing close to the finger-board or the bridge, and strumming the strings to create a variety of tonal colours within the string timbre.

In 'Prelude', which as its name suggests is heard at the start of the film under the credits, a tense dramatic mood is immediately established by five aggressive dissonant *sforzando* (strongly accented) chords whose 'stabbing' sound immediately anticipates the central scene of the film. The music that then follows can only be described as emotionally unsettling, creating anxiety through the use of the following: the furious tempo (*allegro molto agitato*—lively and fast and very agitated); dissonant 7th and 9th chords; ostinato figures; driving rhythms; and swelling, legato melodic phrases.

An important feature of the music and a characteristic of Herrmann's composing style is the use of short motives (rather than longer themes) that are repeated, varied and developed throughout the film to create structural links. For example, the rising semitone figure in bars 3–4 which serves as an ostinato in 'Prelude' is later associated with Marion when sections of the 'Prelude' music are used to accompany her panic-stricken drive to Fairville. A second four-note motive, heard in bars 5–6 over the first ostinato-motive, is also used later in association with Marion.

Study the excerpt of the score of the opening eight bars of 'Prelude' given below and become familiar with the various musical ideas. Then listen to the music, noting the musical means mentioned above that are used to create a feeling of anxiety. (You should also view the scenes of the film in which the music accompanies Marion's anxious drive. The constant rhythms not only complement the car's relentless forward motion; in one scene they are also cleverly synchronised to the to-and-fro movement of the windscreen wipers.)

'The Murder', the music used in the shower scene where Marion appears to be stabbed to death by Norman's mother, is probably the most famous piece of film music ever written. Bernard Herrmann chose one word to describe the significance of the sequence: 'terror'. The music is brilliantly simple, consisting basically of high-pitched screeching dissonant string sounds played forcibly *sul ponticello* (on the bridge). The resulting 'slashes' are not only closely related to visual and aural aspects of the scene—the stabbing motion of the attacker's knife and the victim's screams—they also suggest the shrieks of birds and give us a clue as to the identity of the killer. (The walls of Norman's motel office are lined with stuffed birds.)

Listen to 'The Murder', following the 'Listening outline' on the page opposite.

Opening bars of 'Prelude' from Psycho

Bernard Herrmann

After viewing a rough cut of *Psycho* in December 1959, Hitchcock believed the film would be a failure and was going to get rid of it by editing it into an hour-long show for television. Herrmann begged him to wait until he heard the score. Hitchcock agreed, on the strict condition that the composer wrote no music for the shower scene. Herrmann, however, had silently disagreed with Hitchcock about this scene and proceeded to write what has become his most famous piece. On hearing the final score, Hitchcock changed his mind about the film and was especially impressed by the murder music, which he agreed to include.

Listening outline

A .... First violins play a series of strongly bowed E♭s in their upper register; they are then joined a bar later by the second violins playing E, a major 7th lower, creating a harsh, dissonant effect. Violas, cellos and basses repeat the process so that the major 7th interval is sounding throughout the whole string orchestra

A¹ .... Similar to the first except that the E♭s and Es are now preceded by glissandos, creating a more dissonant, unsettling effect and heightening the terror

B .... Middle-register chords, alternatively bowed and plucked, drop suddenly to heavy sustained octaves on low cellos and basses, suggesting Marion falling and sliding down the shower wall

COMPOSER PROFILE

Bernard Herrmann (1911–75) is considered one of the most original and distinctive composers in all film music. He began his prolific career writing scores for Orson Welles's radio shows in the 1930s and made his film debut in 1941 with the score of *Citizen Kane* (directed by Welles). The most notable of his 40-plus scores were for master English director Alfred Hitchcock, with whom he collaborated on eight films, including *The Man Who Knew Too Much* (1956), *Vertigo* (1958), *North by Northwest* (1959) and *Psycho* (1960). His last score was for the Martin Scorsese film *Taxi Driver*, released in 1976. Herrmann was a master at evoking subtle psychological insights and dramatic tension through music, often using unorthodox instrumental combinations to suit the dramatic needs of a film.

THE BASIC PLOT of *Psycho*

Marion Crane (Janet Leigh) is a Phoenix office worker who is unhappy with her life. She cannot marry her lover, Sam Loomis (John Gavin), as he is too poor to divorce his wife. One Friday Marion is entrusted to bank $40 000 by her boss, a real-estate agent, but instead she leaves town, driving off to Sam's store in Fairville, California with the intention of using the money to start a new life. Fatigued by the long drive and caught in a storm, she leaves the main highway and pulls into the Bates Motel, which is managed by Norman Bates (Anthony Perkins), a quiet but odd young man who appears to be dominated by his mother. After talking with Norman she realises she has made a mistake in stealing the money and decides to return to Phoenix and set matters straight. Unfortunately, Norman's insanely jealous 'mother' has other plans, and Marion is stabbed to death while taking a shower in her motel room. When Marion fails to contact her sister a search begins involving Sam, a private detective hired to recover the money (who is also killed) and the local sheriff. After some dramatic scenes in the Bates's creepy Victorian mansion behind the motel, the shocking identity of the true murderer is revealed.

'LOVE IS IN THE AIR'

from *STRICTLY BALLROOM*

(GEORGE YOUNG & HARRY VANDA)

The 1992 film *Strictly Ballroom* is one of Australia's most successful films, both nationally and overseas. A colourful, funny, sad and exuberant film full of 'over-the-top' characters and featuring spectacular costumes and some excellent dancing (especially by the lead Paul Mercurio), *Strictly Ballroom* is set in the cocooned, glittery and often bizarre world of ballroom dancing, a world rigidly controlled by an establishment (the Ballroom Confederation) that tries to ensure that no new steps are introduced into the traditional dances. As is to be expected, the musical score is made up of songs and musical pieces of various styles to which the characters dance the 'set' steps, such as the waltz and the rhumba. The film is basically a love story involving two characters, Scott and Fran, who rebel against the strict rules of the Ballroom Confederation and bring new steps into the set dances.

'Love Is in the Air', a hit song from 1978 sung in the film by its original singer, Australian John Paul Young, occurs at the end of the film after Scott and Fran have danced in the Pan Pacific Championships. The song, in a **disco** style (see page 131), uses an AABC phrase structure for the verse and an AB structure for the chorus. It conveys a number of emotions, including happiness, exhilaration and romantic love, through the use of the bright major key, lively rhythmic ostinatos, soaring string counter melodies, tubular bells, and backing vocalists in the chorus sections.

Learn to sing 'Love Is in the Air' in the *Score Book*, then listen to it following the 'Listening outline' below.

Listening outline

Introduction	In triple metre. Ascending pitch on synthesiser, strings and piano creates a dreamy mood in preparation for the words 'Love Is in the Air'; descending piano glissando
Verse 1	In quadruple metre. Commences with voice, low-pitched strings, cor anglais counter melody, ascending crotchet arpeggio figure and descending melodic idea; the various rhythms comprising the characteristic disco beat enter in turn—semiquaver pattern on tambourine, snare drum backbeat and finally crotchet beat-pattern on bass drum with the bass guitar playing ♩. ♪♩♩
Verse 2	Continuation in the disco style; ends with an imperfect cadence, chord V being extended with an ascending scale on strings and tubular bells to heighten the emotional feeling
Chorus	Call-and-response between the singer/backing group and strings with tubular bells
Verse 3	As for Verse 2 but with added high string counter melody and low synthesiser ostinato figure
Verse 4	
Chorus	Repeated twice
Coda	Repetition of **hook** (the key phrase—'Love Is in the Air')

Strictly Ballroom's **plot grew from a 50-minute stage play, which started out as a student project at NIDA (the National Institute for the Dramatic Arts). It toured nationally to great acclaim and won awards at an international competition in Czechoslovakia. The Australian producers were unable to convince overseas distributors or financiers to help fund the film, so they turned to their own devices for fund-raising, and made it 'their way'.**

DISCO MUSIC

During the 1970s, discotheques—nightspots where young people could go and dance to the latest recorded hits—became very popular. These discotheques, or 'discos' for short, consisted essentially of a dance floor, a turntable for playing records, a DJ (disc jockey) and his or her mike, and a light show with a mirror ball to create the necessary atmosphere. Gradually a style of music evolved that became associated with these nightspots and the term disco was used for the music that was played there. However, like rock 'n' roll, disco meant more than just the music: it also signified the high-energy dancing, the elegant fashion and the 'underground' setting of dazzling and pulsating coloured lights.

The disco 'sound' consisted of a fast, basic 'beat' of three patterns (given below), with loud bass drum and bass guitar emphasising each beat of the bar. Songs were lavishly produced and often featured harmony singing and soaring string counter melodies for a refined effect. The style was quite flexible and all kinds of songs could be adapted to it. Even classical music, such as Beethoven's Fifth Symphony, received the disco treatment. Disco evolved through the '70s, embracing many dance styles, such as the 'hustle' that applied the techniques of ballroom dancing, and Latin styles that emphasised percussion instruments like cowbells and timbales.

Popular disco bands and artists included K.C. and the Sunshine Band, ABBA, and The Village People, as well as the Bee Gees whose music was featured in the 1977 hit film *Saturday Night Fever*, starring John Travolta (pictured above).

The disco beat

Hi-hats

Snare drum

Bass drum

THE BASIC PLOT
of *Strictly Ballroom*

Champion ballroom dancer Scott Hastings (Paul Mercurio) wants to dance his own steps but this is resisted strongly by the Australian ballroom dance establishment, including the autocratic Chairman Barry Fife (Bill Hunter) and Scott's lifetime dancing parents who are counting on him to fulfil their unrealised ambitions. After his regular dance partner leaves him because of his unorthodox style, Scott teams up with Fran (Tara Morice), a beginning dancer of Spanish heritage whose enthusiasm and eagerness to learn far outweigh her rather plain appearance. As they practice, the two fall in love and Scott learns about 'real' dancing from Fran's father who is an accomplished flamenco dancer. Together Fran and Scott try to win the Pan Pacific Championships and prove to the Ballroom Confederation that they are wrong when they declare, 'There are no new steps!'

 Practical activity

Play on appropriate instruments the rhythmic patterns that make up the disco beat to the verses and chorus of 'Love Is in the Air'. Improvise variations on these patterns for variety.

ARRANGING A SONG

In the performance of 'Love Is in the Air' from *Strictly Ballroom* the basic elements of an arrangement were identified. These are: (1) melody; (2) counter melody; (3) chordal accompaniment; (4) bass line; and (5) percussion accompaniment. A simple arrangement of an eight-bar song involving these five elements is given opposite for you to perform. Refer to this arrangement as you read the notes below.

Writing a simple long-note counter melody

As you heard in 'Love Is in the Air', an instrumental counter melody adds interest and variety to the song. It will usually contrast with the main melody, having a different contour and a rhythm containing long notes. The counter melody must be based on the chord progression of the main melody but must use different notes. Effective long-note counter melodies usually move smoothly, by step as much as possible. (See the counter melody in the 'Sample arrangement' on page 133.)

Writing a bass line

The simplest kind of bass part consists of the root note of each triad in the chord progression played to a particular repeated rhythmic pattern.

This pattern can of course be varied, with other triad notes used on the weak beats. For example, in 'Love Is in the Air', the bass guitar plays

You will notice that the first three notes are the root of the triad and the fourth note is the 5th of the triad (except in bar 4 where it is the 3rd). The 'Sample arrangement' has a similar bass line. Note that in bars 2 and 7 the 3rd of the triad is used on beat 4 to lead to the first note of the next bar. In bar 6, the climax, the 3rd of the triad is used on beat 3 because all parts pause on this beat.

Note on the chordal accompaniment

The triads in bars 2, 4 and 7 do not have the root as the lowest note. They have been rearranged for ease of playing on a keyboard.

Written activities

1. Set the words below from the poem 'Night' by William Blake to an eight-bar melody then arrange it with a long-note counter melody, chordal accompaniment, bass line and percussion. Set out the score as in the 'Sample arrangement' and have it performed by your class.

   The sun descending in the west,
   The evening star does shine;
   The birds are silent in their nest,
   And I must seek for mine.

2. Write a 16-bar song to the words on page 126, Written activity no. 4. Then arrange it for available instruments to include a long-note counter melody, chordal accompaniment, bass line and percussion.

Sample arrangement

'THEME FROM SCHINDLER'S LIST'

from *SCHINDLER'S LIST* (JOHN WILLIAMS)

◀ *Liam Neeson as Oskar Schindler protects a Jewish child from a Nazi soldier in Schindler's List*

American director Steven Spielberg's 1993 epic, *Schindler's List*, is a moving and highly personalised film set amidst the horrors of the Holocaust—the killing of 6 000 000 Jews by the Nazis in the Second World War. Based on the novel by Australian author Thomas Keneally, the film is not, however, simply another harrowing account of this dark chapter of history. It tells the uplifting story of the rich Czech-born businessman Oskar Schindler, initially a Nazi-sympathiser, who gradually becomes so affected by the plight of the Jewish workers in his Polish enamelware factory that he ends up saving over a thousand of them from the gas chambers. Photographed mainly in black-and-white (to capture the grim tone of the subject matter), the film won seven Oscars, including one for Best Original Score.

Once again Spielberg chose composer John Williams for his film, and the resulting music perfectly complements the pathos of the visual images. The award-winning score is notable for its quiet dignity, its emotional intensity, its melodic beauty and its effective use of the solo violin. The choice of this instrument is a fitting one, as the violin is considered to be the instrument most capable of expressing human emotions. It is also the instrument most associated today with Jewish music. (Many of the world's greatest violinists are Jewish, such as Itzhak Perlman who plays the solos on the film's soundtrack.) In *Schindler's List* the violin thus takes on the symbolic role of the voice of the Jewish nation, commenting on and reacting to the tragic and horrific situations. This is evident in the famous main 'Theme', the melody of which (given below) so brilliantly expresses the deep sorrow and despair of the persecuted Jews. It is heard briefly a number of times during the film and in its entirety at the end when the Jewish survivors and their descendants place stones on Schindler's tomb in Israel as a mark of honour.

The sorrow expressed in the 'Theme' is achieved through several means, including the slow tempo, the minor key, the dark, mournful timbre of the cor anglais, the lonely sound of the solo violin, the mainly string accompaniment (which, as we saw in *Psycho*, creates a bleak effect and matches the black-and-white photography), and the repeated two-note downward-falling motive of the melody that recurs throughout, widening as it progresses. (The use of wide intervals produces an unsettled feeling and is often a feature of themes of yearning.) Adding poignancy to the music are the dissonances created by the non-chordal melody notes used on strong beats, for example the notes marked with an asterisk in bars 1, 3 and 4 of the music below, and by the non-chordal notes used in the inner

voices (the counter melodies and string chords). The emotion is further heightened by the frequent expressive performance directions, indicated in the score by such terms as *dim.* (*diminuendo*— becoming softer), *cresc.* (*crescendo*—becoming louder), *rall.* (*rallentando*—gradually becoming slower), *rit.* (*ritenuto*—immediately becoming slower) and *a tempo* (return to the former speed).

Learn to play the melody of the 'Theme' then listen to a piano performance of it, following the score in the *Score Book*. (This version is heard at the end of the film, under the credits.) Observe the way the repeated two-note motive is used—twice with perfect 5ths, twice with major 6ths and once with a minor 7th—and try to locate examples of non-chordal notes in the inner melodies. (You will find some in bars 2, 6 and 8.) Notice how these dissonances heighten the emotional effect of the music. After you have studied the piano score, listen to the orchestral performance of the 'Theme' while following the 'Listening outline' on page 136.

Schindler's List **won seven Oscars for Best Picture, Director, Adapted Screenplay, Art Direction, Cinematography, Editing and Original Score.**

'Theme from Schindler's List'

John Williams

Listening outline

Introduction Cor anglais melody accompanied by sustained strings and harp chords

A .... Theme on solo violin accompanied by strings and harp with cor anglais counter melodies

A¹ .... Theme on solo violin an octave higher

B .... Theme on lower strings played in their upper register. Solo violin plays counter melodies

B¹ .... Violin plays the theme. Flute counter melodies

A²

Coda

THE BASIC PLOT of *Schindler's List*

Czech-born Oskar Schindler (Liam Neeson), a vain, woman-ising and greedy businessman, makes a fortune at the start of the Second World War by using cheap Jewish labour in his enamelware factory in Krakow, Poland and selling his pots and pans to the Germans. In 1943, the Ghetto, the section of Krakow where the segregated Jews are forced to live in appalling conditions, is destroyed by the Nazis and many Jews are killed. The survivors are herded into trains for transportation to forced labour camps or to the gas chambers of Auschwitz. Schindler gradually becomes sympathetic to the plight of his workers and secretly schemes to save them. Using his friendship and influence with the local commander Amon Goeth (Ralph Fiennes), a Nazi who shoots Jews for sport, he turns his factory into a refuge and manages to save over 1000 men, women and children from certain death.

'With dignity and compassion, John Williams has composed original and stunningly classical music for *Schindler's List* in a collection of themes and orchestral remembrances that will haunt you. The antihuman events beginning with Kristallnacht (1938) to the liberation of Auschwitz-Birkenau (1944) posed a deliberate challenge to both John and me: how to make the unimaginable factual, and how to create not so much a motion picture but a document of those intolerable times.

The choice John Williams made was gentle simplicity. Most of our films together have required an almost operatic accompaniment, which is fitting for *Indiana Jones*, *Close Encounters*, or *Jaws*. Each of us had to depart from our characteristic styles and begin again. This is certainly an album to be attended with closed eyes and unsequestered hearts.'

STEVEN SPIELBERG
ON THE MUSIC OF *SCHINDLER'S LIST*

MINOR MELODY WRITING

As we saw in the 'Theme' from *Schindler's List*, the use of a minor key is especially appropriate for expressing sorrow. When writing songs, there are many occasions when a minor key is more suitable than a major key, particularly when the lyrics deal with such emotions as sadness, fear, regret or longing. However, in a minor melody special care must be taken with the treatment of the raised leading note in order to avoid awkward intervals that are difficult to sing. One way to solve this problem is to use only another note of chord V, or the tonic note, before or after the leading note, as in the example below.

If you wish to use the sixth, seventh and eighth degrees in succession, a common practice is to raise the sixth degree a semitone (as well as the seventh) going up, and to use the natural minor form of the scale going down (that is, using the unraised leading note). Study examples 1 and 2 opposite. In the first the raised leading note F♯ is approached from E♭ in bar 1 and followed by E♭ in bars 2 and 3, giving intervals of a tone and a half. In the second

Example 1

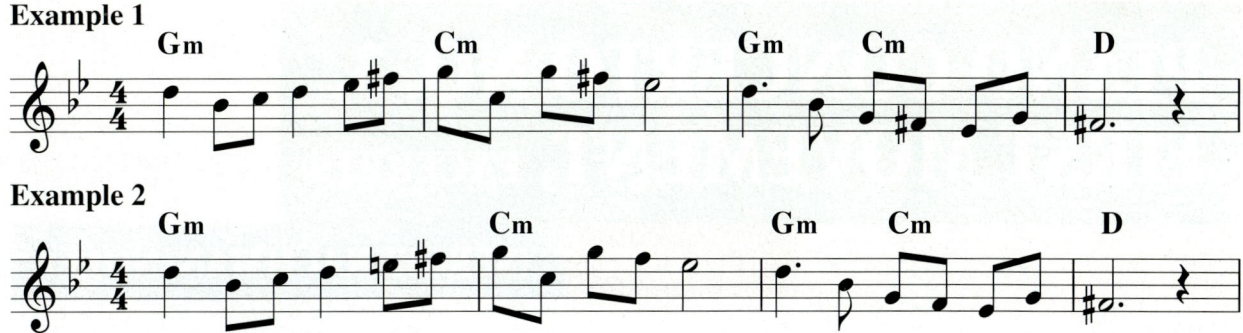

Example 2

example the awkward interval is avoided by raising the 6th in bar 1 and by using the unraised leading note in bars 2 and 3. This produces steps of tones which are easier to sing. Listen to these examples as they are played to you, noting the effect.

Further consideration must be given to the chord progression, since in a minor key chord ii is neither a major nor a minor triad (see page 94) and

would need special treatment. The following chord progression will produce a satisfactory binary-form eight-bar minor melody:

First phrase   I–IV– I – V
Second phrase   I–IV–V7–I

Study the 'Sample eight-bar minor melody' below, then play it with chordal accompaniment.

Sample eight-bar minor melody

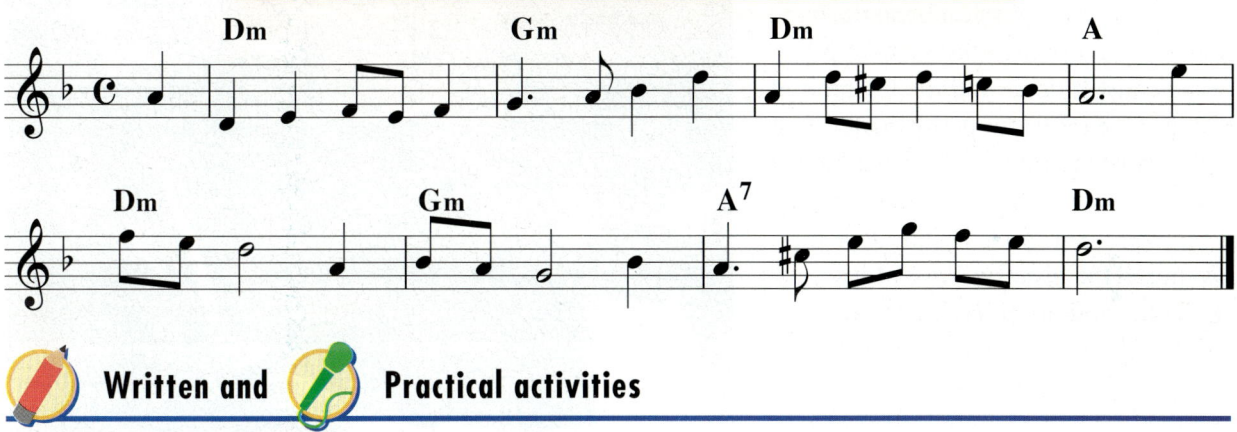

Written and Practical activities

1. Write a melody in D minor using the rhythmic pattern in triple metre on page 125. Play your melody with chordal accompaniment.

2. Set the following words to an eight-bar minor melody in E minor. Include two examples of word painting. Sing your song with chordal accompaniment.

   Farewell, little birdies that fly in the sky,
   That fly all day long and sing troubles by.
   I am doomed to this cell, I heave a deep sigh,
   My heart sinks within me, in anguish I die.

3. Write a 16-bar binary-form composition for a solo instrument with piano accompaniment. The A section should be in a minor key and the B section in a major key (either the relative major or tonic major, for a stronger contrast). The solo part should be basically 2 eight-bar melodies, but can contain figures that would be too difficult for a voice to sing. Add expression terms and signs and perform the composition to the class.

 Aural activity

Notate minor melodies played to you by your teacher.

PIANO CONCERTO NO. 3, FIRST MOVEMENT, EXCERPTS

from *SHINE* (SERGEI RACHMANINOFF)

The 1996 Australian film *Shine*, based on the true-life story of pianist David Helfgott, is one of the most inspiring films ever produced. The film, for which Geoffrey Rush won an Oscar for Best Actor, tells the story of David's early life with his family in Perth in the 1950s; the emotional upheavals caused by the overbearing oppression of his tyrannical father; David's struggles to break free; his time studying at the Royal College of Music in London; his complete mental and physical breakdown that led to more than ten years in psychiatric institutions; and the triumph of his ultimate return to performance. It is a film in which there are conflicting emotions, although the emotion of love is the dominant force: David's love for his music; the obsessive love of his autocratic and domineering father Peter; the love and friendship of the writer Katharine Susannah Prichard; and the love and encouragement of his friend Silvia and his wife Gillian.

Through *Shine* runs the thread of the music of the very difficult Piano Concerto No. 3 in D minor by the early twentieth-century Russian composer Sergei Rachmaninoff. (A **concerto** is a composition written for solo instrument combined with an orchestra.) As a small boy, David learnt to play the main theme of this concerto from listening to a recording and was determined to master the work one day. He finally performs the concerto in the competition he wins in London when on the verge of his breakdown. His tutor, Professor Cecil Parks, has told him that 'performing is a risk … no safety net … it's dangerous', and so it proves for David.

The film does not provide the whole concerto—the opening theme is joined to a number of other sections of the first and third movements—showing

▲ Noah Taylor as the young pianist David Helfgott performing the very difficult Rachmaninoff Concerto No. 3 in the London concerto competition in Shine

David at various times during the momentous performance. The beautiful D minor theme that Rachmaninoff said 'simply wrote itself' is one of those 'heaven-sent' melodies that seems to evolve as it progresses. With its simplicity, mainly stepwise movement, minor tonality and its dark, Russian, folklike quality, it is like a song sung by the piano in unison octaves. The orchestra provides a simple accompaniment with prominent bassoon, cello, and finally woodwind counter melodies. The first nine bars of the theme are given below for you to play.

At bar 29 the melody is taken over by horn and violas while the piano plays semiquaver **broken chord** figures (patterns in which notes of a chord are played one after the other instead of together). Read the 'Score reading notes' below, then listen to the opening section of the concerto, following the score in the *Score Book*.

Theme from Piano Concerto No. 3, first movement

Sergei Rachmaninoff

Score reading notes to Piano Concerto No. 3

1. The piano part is written above the strings, the usual position for a solo instrument in a concerto score.
2. The bassoon music is written in the **tenor clef**, which sets middle C on the fourth line.
3. Violins and violas play semiquaver tremolos indicated by quavers with an added horizontal stroke.
4. In bar 1 (and in other places) only first clarinet, first bassoon and third horn play; the other instrument of each pair has a rest written in the music.
5. From bar 27 the music is divided between the hands, notes with stems going up being played by the right hand and those with stems going down being played by the left hand. Sometimes only one staff is used to avoid too many ledger lines. In such cases no rests are required in the other staff.
6. For the meanings of the many Italian terms used in the score refer to the box on page 140.

THE CADENZA FROM THE FIRST MOVEMENT

Rachmaninoff composed two cadenzas for the first movement, one much more elaborate and difficult than the other. (A cadenza is a free solo section sounding like an improvisation, often based on themes previously heard.) In the film, David is shown playing the difficult **cadenza** for his tutor, who tells him that to play this cadenza he has to imagine each hand has ten fingers. Commencing at the orchestral pause and the word 'ossia' (meaning or), the cadenza features right-hand chords leaping a 3rd, an interval derived from the opening two notes of the theme. These are heard against sextuplets in the left hand, creating cross-rhythms at bars 17–26 and 33–34. At bar 43 both hands, to the same rhythm, play a harmonised rhythmic variation of the theme with thick accented chords. The climax of the cadenza commences at bar 62 and features *fff* dynamics, chords (frequently four notes in each hand) moving in parallel motion, and the use of extreme registers of the piano. At bar 68 an accelerando leads to a low D in the left hand at bar 72, at which point in the film the bass string snaps.

Listen to the cadenza, following the score in the *Score Book*.

Italian terms used in the Rachmaninoff Piano Concerto No. 3

a tempo return to former speed
allegro ma non tanto not too lively and fast
allegro molto very lively and fast
arco play with the bow
colla parte with the solo part
commodo comfortable, that is, at a comfortable, moderate speed
con sord. (con sordini) with mutes
cresc. ed accelerando gradually becoming louder and faster
dolce sweetly
legato smoothly, well connected
più mosso more moved, that is, quicker
pizz. (pizzicato) pluck the string
poco a poco little by little
poco cresc. (poco crescendo) gradually becoming a little louder
presto very fast
rit. (ritenuto) immediately slower, held back

THE BASIC PLOT of *Shine*

Caught in a storm one night, David Helfgott (Geoffrey Rush) seeks refuge in a wine bar. The owner, Sylvia (Sonia Todd) gives the eccentric and brilliant pianist a job playing in the bar. The story of David's early life from the 1950s is then told in flashback. As a young prodigy, David is completely controlled by his domineering and autocratic father (Armin Mueller-Stahl), who wants his son to be a great pianist but is not prepared to let him go his own way and refuses to allow him to study in America. David (now played by Noah Taylor) is befriended and encouraged by the writer Katharine Susannah Prichard (Googie Withers) and when he is offered a scholarship to the Royal College of Music in London he finally defies his father, who from then on refuses to acknowledge him. In London David becomes ever more eccentric as he studies with Professor Cecil Parks (John Gielgud). He finally achieves greatness in the concerto competition playing his beloved 'Rach 3', but has a mental breakdown and returns to Australia where he spends more than ten years in psychiatric institutions. Through his friend Sylvia, David meets the astrologer Gillian (Lynn Redgrave) who eventually marries him; with her love and encouragement he finds the freedom to experience his ecstasy and passion and is finally able to resume his career as a concert pianist.

COMPOSER PROFILE

The Russian-born composer Sergei Rachmaninoff (1873–1943) left Russia in 1917 and spent much of the remainder of his life in America. He was regarded as one of the most brilliant pianists of the early decades of the twentieth century and toured the world extensively. He was also highly respected as a conductor and became well known as a composer with a number of very popular works, including the Prelude in C Sharp minor for piano, the Piano Concerto No. 2 in C minor and the *Variations on a Theme of Paganini* for Piano and Orchestra. Rachmaninoff's Piano Concerto No. 3 was written especially for a tour of America in 1909 in which he appeared as pianist and conductor with the Boston Symphony Orchestra. His compositions include operas, three symphonies, four piano concertos, many pieces for piano solo and songs. Rachmaninoff is considered a late romantic composer, that is, he continued writing in the traditional forms and styles of nineteenth century composers such as Chopin, Liszt and Tchaikovsky.

 ## FILM MUSIC FOR AURAL ANALYSIS

The opening music, 'Anvil of Crom' from *Conan the Barbarian* is a rare example of a piece of film music that fulfils the four functions of a film score that we have studied. A brief background to the film is given below. After you have read this, listen to 'Anvil of Crom' then answer the questions on page 142.

'Anvil of Crom' (Basil Poledouris)

from *Conan the Barbarian*

The 1981 adventure fantasy *Conan the Barbarian*, starring Arnold Schwarzenegger as a powerful sword-wielding warrior (pictured right), is set in an undefined pre-historic age. As a child Conan witnesses the brutal murder of his parents by the evil Thulsa Doom and is chained to the Wheel of Pain. When he is freed many years later, he sets out on a long journey with Subotai the Mongol and Valeria, Queen of Thieves, to seek revenge for the death of his parents. Conan finds the killer Doom at the top of his Mountain of Power and after a number of very narrow escapes he defeats Doom and exacts his just revenge.

Because of the primitive nature of the characters, dialogue is kept to a minimum. To compensate, the film uses music throughout, with various themes being used to suggest an uncivilised European age, create various moods, represent the main characters and express their emotions. Music in *Conan the Barbarian* takes on a greater role than in most films; in fact the director (John Milius) told the composer Basil Poledouris to make his score 'a continuous music drama'. The resulting symphonic score is considered to be one of the most important soundtracks of the 1980s.

The opening sequence, 'Anvil of Crom', is heard at the start of the film as Conan's sword is forged on the anvil. It contains two important themes symbolising the central conflict in the drama which recur throughout the film to unify the different scenes: the energetic first theme (A) representing Conan; and the contrasting second theme (B), known as 'The Riddle of Steel', which is an emotional melody suggesting the idea of Conan's quest. The A-section music is unusual for two reasons: (1) it features changing metres of six and five beats to the bar; and (2) it is scored for 24 French horns, strings and percussion. 'Anvil of Crom' fulfils the four functions of a film score that we have studied: (1) it sets the time and place (pre-historic Europe); (2) it creates a dramatic mood; (3) it portrays Conan's character; and (4) it expresses his emotions (in 'The Riddle of Steel').

Listening questions

1. What is the form of the 'Anvil of Crom'? (Use letters.)
2. What two features of the A section evoke the feeling of a primitive civilisation?
3. What aspects of Conan's character are portrayed in this music? (Mention at least two.) How are they portrayed?
4. What kind of mood is created in the A section music? What musical features help create this mood?
5. What musical means are used in the B section to express Conan's yearning for his quest?

WORDS TO KNOW

melisma	Dorian mode
monophonic	hornpipe
texture	transposing
polyphonic	instrument
texture	disco
homophonic	concerto
texture	broken chord
jig	cadenza
reel	tenor clef

Activities for senior students

Composition

Imagine you are composing music to accompany an emotional film scene. Write a short description of the scene and decide on the emotion(s) that need to be expressed. Compose an appropriate piece of music for your scene, taking into consideration such elements as timbre, texture, tonality, harmony, consonance/dissonance, melodic contour, rhythm, dynamics and so on.

Arranging

Select a piece of film music that expresses a particular emotion, for example 'Tara's Theme' from *Gone With the Wind*, and arrange it for available instruments, ensuring that your orchestration contributes to the expression of the emotion.

Create a soundtrack

Find an appropriate piece of recorded music to express an emotion in a particular film scene. Dub the music onto the film.

Research activity

Select a film in which the music expresses varying emotions, for example *Cry Freedom* or *Shadowlands*—both of which have scores by George Fenton. Select at least three different pieces used in the film and analyse the composer's use of musical elements to express the emotions. You will need to quote the musical themes to which you are referring.

Oral presentation

Choose three films with scores by different composers in which the music helps to express the same emotion, for example happiness or terror. Using video excerpts compare and contrast each composer's use of musical elements to express the emotion.

APPENDIXES

Solfa hand signs

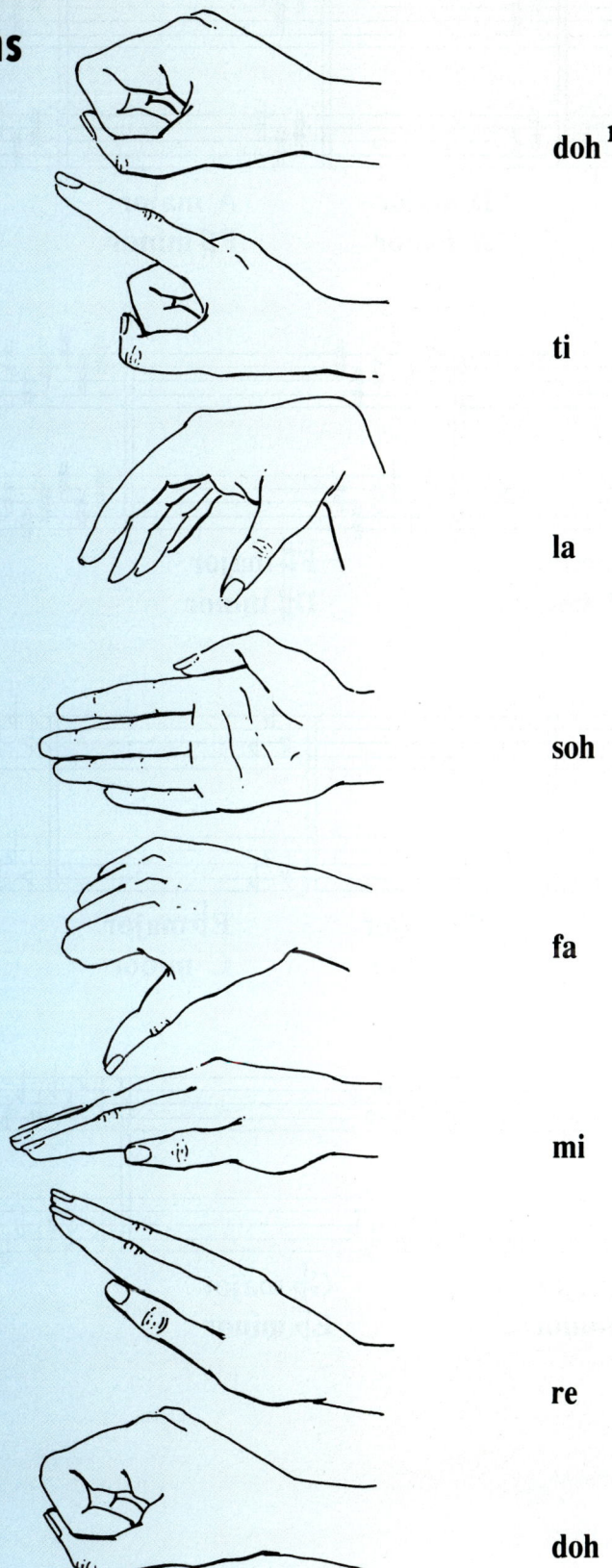

doh[1]

ti

la

soh

fa

mi

re

doh

Major and minor key signatures

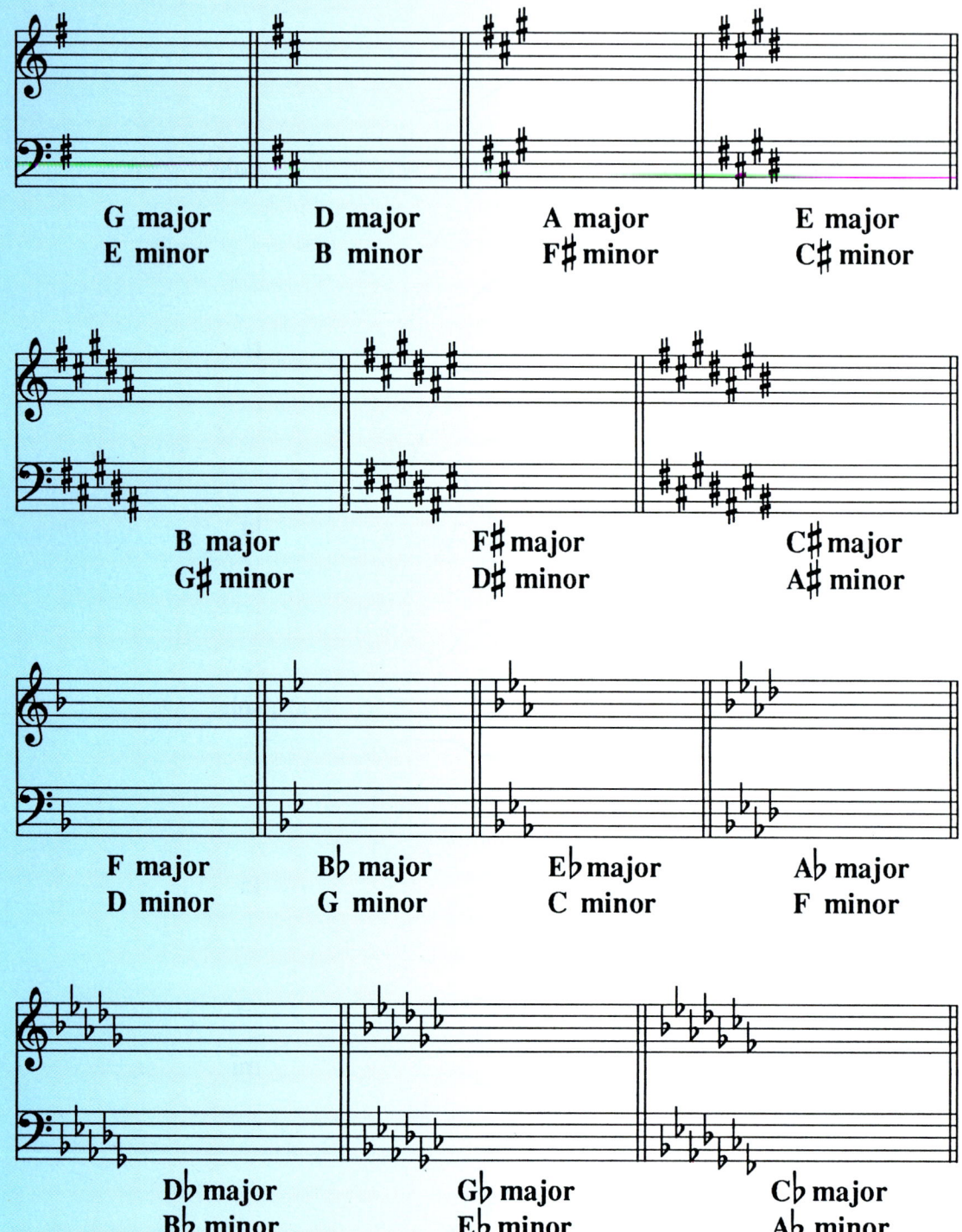

G major   D major   A major   E major
E minor   B minor   F♯ minor   C♯ minor

B major   F♯ major   C♯ major
G♯ minor   D♯ minor   A♯ minor

F major   B♭ major   E♭ major   A♭ major
D minor   G minor   C minor   F minor

Db major   Gb major   Cb major
Bb minor   Eb minor   Ab minor

Recorder fingering chart

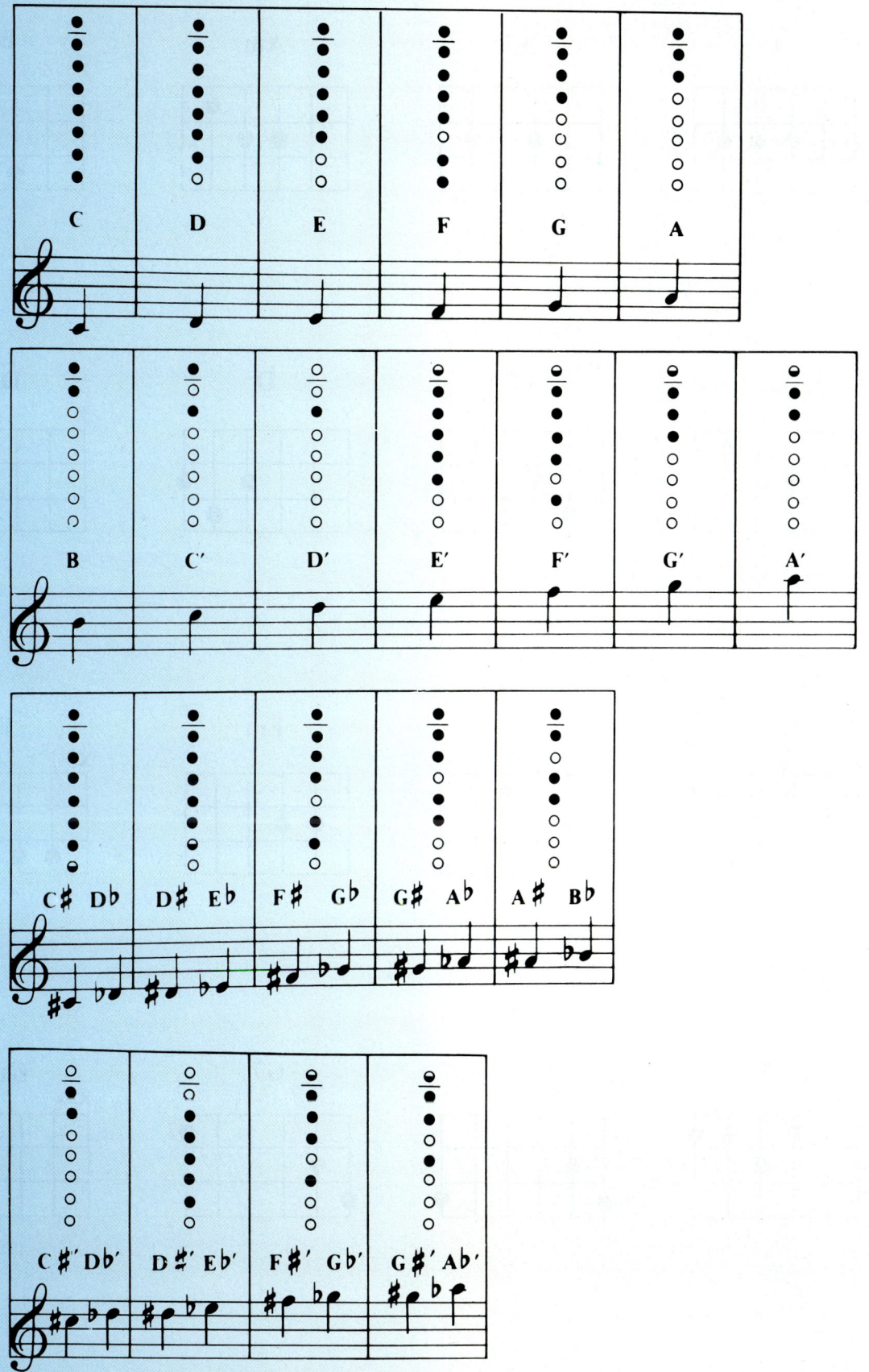

Guitar chord chart

A
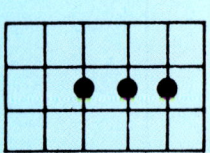

A7
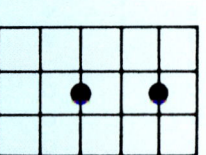

Am
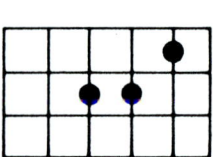

B♭
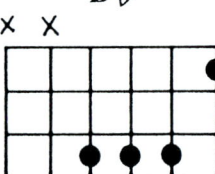

C
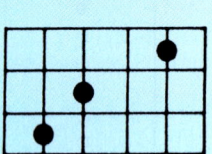

C7
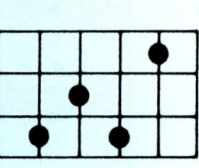

D
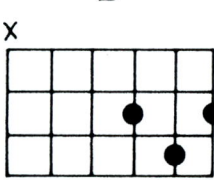

D7
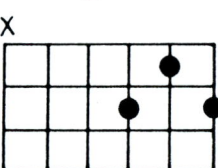

Dm
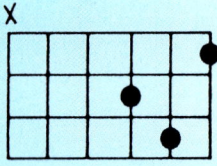

E7
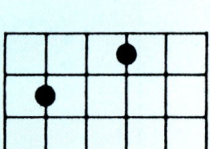

Em
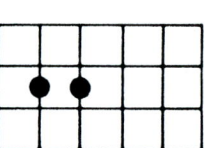

F
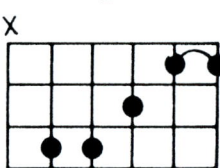

F7
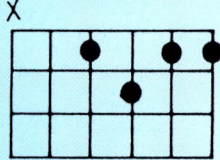

G
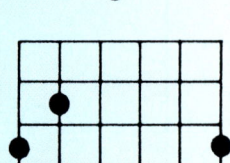

G7
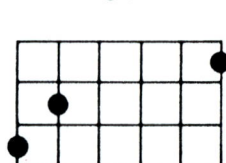

Gm
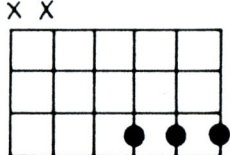

Practical instrument ranges

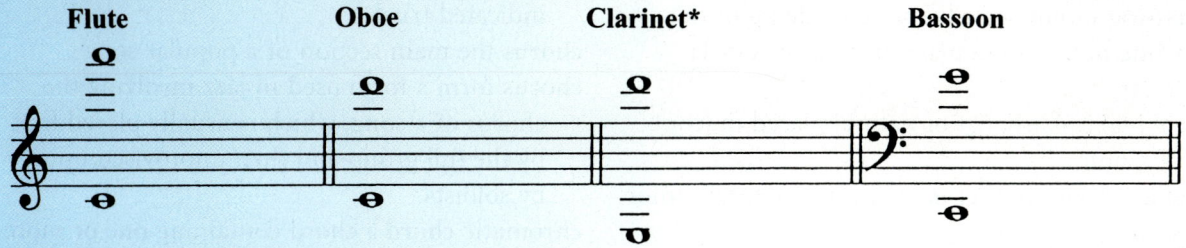

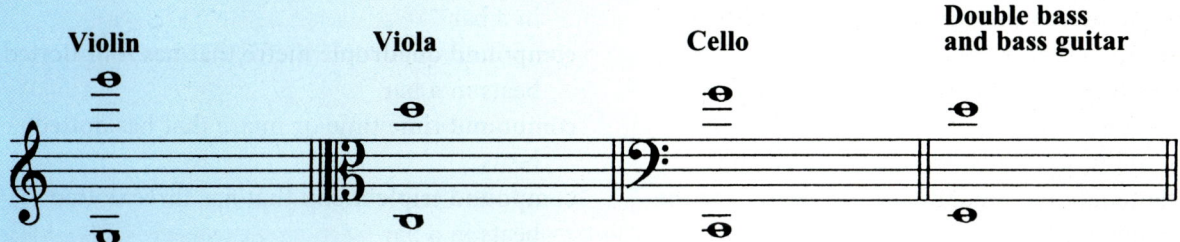

* Transposes down a major 2nd
** Transposes down a perfect 5th

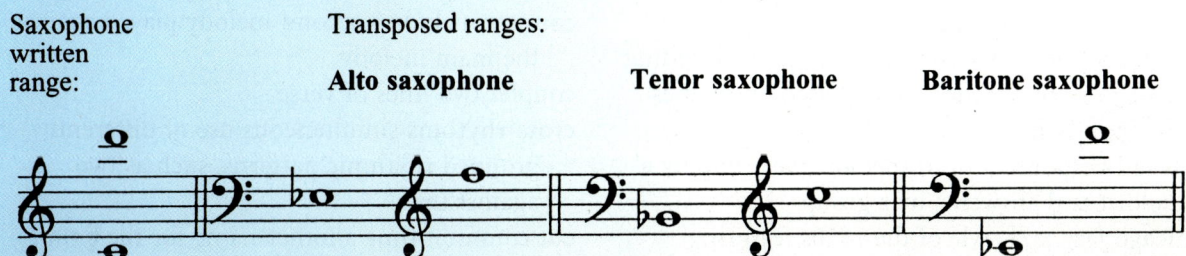

GLOSSARY

A natural minor scale the scale made up of the white notes of the piano from A to A or la to la[1]

accidental a sharp, flat or natural placed in front of a note

Aeolian mode another name for the natural minor scale

alto clef sign 𝄡 at the beginning of a staff, giving the letter name 'middle C' to the third line

appoggiatura an ornament that takes the accent and part of the time value of the main note

articulation the attack and release of the notes, e.g. staccato, legato, accent

atonal music that does not have a key

avant garde a term used to describe the works of composers of the second part of the twentieth century who have broken away from the conventional treatment of musical elements and have invented entirely new compositional techniques

baroque period the period of musical history from 1600 to 1750

binary form a formal structure involving two sections: AB

blue notes notes used in jazz, produced by flattening the 3rd, 5th and 7th degrees of the major scale

blues chord progression a 12-bar arrangement of chords: I I I I IV IV I I V V I I

broken chord a pattern in which the notes of a chord are played one after the other instead of together

cadence a progression of two chords where the music comes to a point of rest

cadenza a free solo section in a concerto sounding like an improvisation, often based on themes previously heard

call-and-response a short melodic idea sung by a soloist and answered by a group

Chicago jazz jazz style of the 1920s featuring small instrumental groups

chord two or more notes of different pitch sounding together

chord progression chords used in a piece of music or a section of music that are arranged in a particular order

chord symbol the letter name of the root of a triad written above a melody to indicate the chord to be played

chordal note a melody note that belongs to the indicated triad

chorus the main section of a popular song

chorus form a form used in jazz involving the chorus of a song, which is usually played first by the full group and then improvised upon by soloists

chromatic chord a chord containing one or more chromatic notes

chromatic note a note foreign to the key

chromatic scale a scale that moves by semitone steps

classical period the period of musical history from 1750 to 1825, characterised by balance and order

common time four crotchet beats in the bar, shown by the time signature 𝄴

complex metre an irregular metre that is made up of a combination of two-beat and three-beat patterns such as $\frac{5}{4}$ or $\frac{7}{8}$

compound duple metre that has two dotted beats in a bar

compound quadruple metre that has four dotted beats in a bar

compound time time or metre that has dotted beats

compound triple metre that has three dotted beats in a bar

concerto a composition written for a solo instrument combined with an orchestra

concord a chord that is pleasant to the ear and seems to be at rest. Made up of intervals of a 3rd, 4th, 5th, 6th and 8ve

contour the shape of a melody (smooth/angular)

counter melody a second melody played against the main melody

couplet two lines of verse

cross-rhythms simultaneous use of differently grouped rhythmic patterns, such as two against three

cut common time another name for the $\frac{2}{2}$ time signature (in which there are two minim beats to the bar), indicated by 𝄵

disco a style of dance music popular in the 1970s

discord a chord that is jarring on the ear and does not sound at rest. Made up of intervals of a 2nd and a 7th

dissonant harmony discordant harmony (see discord)

dominant the fifth degree of the scale

Dorian mode a scale with a different arrangement of tones and semitones from that of the major scale, corresponding to the white notes of the piano from D to D¹

drone a note, or notes, of fixed pitch continuing throughout a section of music

duple metre two beats in the bar

duration the length of a sound

dynamics the degree of loudness or softness of music, indicated by terms or signs in the score

epic a large-scale 'blockbuster' film dealing with the adventures of an heroic individual

flat the sign ♭ placed in front of a note which lowers the note one semitone

glissando a sliding pitch effect

harmonic minor scale another name for the minor scale (with a raised leading note)

harmonic rhythm the frequency with which the chords change in a piece

harmony the general term used for the chords in a piece of music

homophonic texture a melodic line heard against a chordal accompaniment

hornpipe a lively dance in $\frac{4}{4}$ time common in Celtic music, often associated with sailors

imitation the repetition of a melodic pattern by a different instrumental line or 'voice'

imperfect cadence a cadence formed by the chord progression I–V which does not give a feeling of finality

interval the distance in pitch between two notes

jig a lively country dance in $\frac{6}{8}$ time common in Celtic music

key the name of the scale on which a piece of music is based

key signature the sharps or flats written after the clef that belong to the scale on which a piece of music is based

leading note the seventh degree of the scale

major interval the quality of the interval formed between the tonic and the second, third, sixth and seventh degrees of the major scale

major scale a series of eight notes in alphabetical order that, ascending, produces the following pattern of tones and semitones: T T S T T T S

major triad a triad containing a major 3rd and a perfect 5th above the root

medieval period the period of musical history from 450 to 1450

melisma the use of two or more notes to a word or syllable in a melody, indicated by a slur

melodic ostinato a short repeated melodic idea

military band style a style of music written for a band made up of different types of woodwind, brass and percussion instruments and featuring bright tempo, two-beat metre, two-beat oom-pah bass played by tuba and lively rhythms

minor interval an interval that is a semitone smaller than a major interval

minor scale a scale in which the semitones occur between the second and third, fifth and sixth, and seventh and eighth degrees

minor triad a triad containing a minor 3rd and a perfect 5th above the root

Mixolydian mode a scale with a different arrangement of tones and semitones from that of the major scale, corresponding to the white notes of the piano from G to G¹

monophonic texture one line of music heard by itself

natural the sign ♮ placed in front of a note that cancels the effect of a sharp or flat

non-chordal note a melody note that does not belong to the indicated triad

orchestral score the written music for an orchestra

ornamentation the use of added notes to decorate a melody

ostinato a repeated rhythmic pattern

pedal note a long held or repeated bass note against which the harmony changes

pentatonic scale a five-note scale sung to the solfa syllables doh, re, mi, soh, and la

perfect cadence a cadence formed by the chord progression V–I which gives a feeling of finality

perfect intervals the quality of the interval formed between the tonic and its unison, the fourth, the fifth and the eighth degrees of a major or minor scale

pitch the highness or lowness of a sound

plagal cadence a cadence formed by the chord progression IV–I

polyphonic texture two or more melodic lines moving independently but heard together

polyrhythms different rhythms heard simultaneously

primary triads the triads built on the first, fourth and fifth degrees of the scale

quadruple metre four beats in the bar

ragtime a piano music style popular from the 1890s to 1930s featuring a structure comprising three or four contrasting sections often repeated, a bright march tempo, duple metre, regular left-hand rhythm and a syncopated right-hand melody

range the distance in pitch between the lowest and highest notes of a melody

reel a fast dance with smoothly flowing rhythm in duple or quadruple metre common in Celtic music, danced by two or more couples facing each other

relative major and minor major and minor keys that have the same key signature

riff a repeated rhythmic/melodic phrase

renaissance period the period of musical history from 1450 to 1600

rock 'n' roll a 1950s rock style that featured the used of small instrumental groups consisting of amplified acoustic guitars, double bass, saxophone and drums, and that was characterised by a frenzied, raucous sound and a strong beat for dancing

romantic period the period of musical history from 1825 to 1900 characterised by emotion and individualism

rondo form a formal structure involving at least five sections: ABACA

root the lowest note of a triad

scale a series of notes arranged in pitch order

scale degrees the position of each note in the scale, counting upwards from the lowest note

score the printed music

semitone the smallest interval between two notes on the keyboard

sequence the repetition of a pattern at a different pitch level

seventh chord a triad with an extra note, a 7th above the root, to add extra harmonic colour

sextuplet six notes played in the time of four of the same value

sharp the sign ♯ placed in front of a note that raises the note one semitone

simple duple a time signature that has two undotted beats in a bar

simple quadruple a time signature that has four undotted beats in a bar

simple time time or metre that has simple, undotted beats

simple triple a time signature that has three undotted beats in a bar

spiritual a religious song of the African-Americans whose ancestors were transported to North America as slaves

staccato short and detached; indicated by dots under or over the notes

string quartet an instrumental group comprising two violins, viola and cello

swing big-band jazz style popular from 1930 to 1945

symphonic poem a programmatic orchestral composition with a number of descriptive sections

symphony a large instrumental work for orchestra, which usually has four movements

syncopation accenting a beat or part of a beat that is not normally accented

tempo the speed of the music, indicated by terms in the score

tenor clef sign 𝄡 at the beginning of a staff, giving the letter name 'middle C' to the fourth line

ternary form a formal structure involving three sections: ABA

texture the thickness of the sound

theme short phrases or melodies representing a person, place, object, animal or idea

timbre the tone colour of a sound

tone the interval of two semitones together

tone cluster a band of sounds produced by notes sung or played very close together

tonic the first degree of the scale

transposing instrument an instrument on which the player produces a note that sounds at a particular interval above or below the written note

triad a three-note chord consisting of a root, the lowest note, plus a 3rd and a 5th above it

trill a rapid alternation of a note with the note above it

triple metre three beats in the bar

triplet three notes played in the time of two of the same value

unison the interval formed by two notes of the same pitch

volume the loudness or softness of a sound

whole-tone scale a scale that moves by tones

word painting the use of a musical element to depict the meaning of the lyrics

ACKNOWLEDGMENTS

MUSIC

The Man from Snowy River II
Themes from 'The Chase' (Bruce Rowland)
Music by Bruce Rowland reproduced by
permission Festival Music Pty. Limited;

The Man from Snowy River
'Theme' (Bruce Rowland)
Music by Bruce Rowland reproduced by
permission Festival Music Pty. Limited;

Red River
Cattle theme and Red River theme from 'Red
River Crossing' (Dmitri Tiomkin)
Warner Chappell;

Murder on the Orient Express
'Waltz' (Richard Rodney Bennett)
Reprinted with permission from G. Schirmer
(Aust) Pty Ltd;

Tous les Matins du Monde
'Turkish March' from *Le Bourgeois
Gentilhomme* (Jean-Baptiste Lully)
© Furstner-Boosey & Hawkes. Reproduced by
permission;

Born Free
'Born Free' (John Barry)
By permission EMI Music Publishing Australia
Pty Ltd;

The Piano
'The Heart Asks Pleasure First' (Michael
Nyman)
Reprinted with permission from G. Schirmer
(Aust) Pty Ltd;

Patton
'Patton Theme' (Jerry Goldsmith)
Warner Chappell;

Raiders of the Lost Ark
'The Raiders March' (John Williams)
© 1981 Ensign Music Corporation USA. All
rights reserved. International copyright secured.
Permission granted by Music Sales Pty Ltd;

Emma
'Main Titles' (Rachel Portman)
Written and composed by Rachel Portman
(BMI) 100% Miramax Film Music (Adm by
Sony/ATV Songs LLC) (BMI) 100% © 1996;

G.I. Blues
'Blue Suede Shoes' (Carl Lee Perkins)
© Melody reprinted with permission of J.
Albert & Son Pty Ltd. All rights reserved;

The Mission
'River' (Ennio Morricone)
By permission EMI Music Publishing Australia
Pty Ltd;
'Gabriel's Oboe' (Ennio Morricone)
By permission EMI Music Publishing Australia
Pty Ltd;

Henry V
'Non Nobis, Domine' (Patrick Doyle)
Warner Chappell;

Gone with the Wind
'Tara's Theme' (Max Steiner)
Warner Chappell;

Psycho
'Prelude' (Bernard Herrmann)
©1960 Famous Music Corporation, USA All
rights reserved. International copright secured.
Permission granted by Music Sales Pty Ltd;

Schindler's List
'Theme from *Schindler's List*' (John Williams)
Warner Chappell.

PHOTOGRAPHS

The Kobal Collection (*The Kid*);
Australian Picture Library (galloping horses);
Bruce Rowland (photo of himself);
The Photo Library, Sydney (symphony orchestra);
The Kobal Collection (*Braveheart*, Andrew
    Cooper, Paramount Pictures, © 1995 BH
    Finance CV);
The Performing Arts Library (African drums,
    Baaba Maal and Daande, Womad 1995,
    © Steve Gillett);
The Kobal Collection (*The Last Emperor*);
The Performing Arts Library (Chinese musicians,
    © Jane Mont);
The Kobal Collection (*Red River*);
Black Star (Dmitri Tiomkin, © 1997 David Khan);

The Kobal Collection (*The Sting*);

The Kobal Collection (*Murder on The Orient Express*);

Novello & Co (Richard Rodney Bennett, photo by Sasha Gusow);

Cinesound Movietone Productions Pty Ltd (*On Our Selection*);

Australian Picture Library (Palace of Versailles, photo by Arthur Hustwitt);

Performing Arts Library (theorbos, © Clive Barda);

The Kobal Collection (*Forrest Gump*, © 1994 Paramount Pictures);

The Kobal Collection (*Dr No*);

The Kobal Collection (*Those Magnificent Men in Their Flying Machines*);

The Kobal Collection (*Born Free*);

Australian Picture Library (Michael Nyman, © Matt Anker);

The Kobal Collection (*Patton*);

The Kobal Collection (*Indiana Jones and the Temple of Doom*);

Australian Picture Library/Corbis Bettman (John Williams);

The Kobal Collection (*Emma*, © 1995 Miramax Films, photo by David Appleby);

National Film and Sound Archive (*My Brilliant Career*);

Australian Picture Library/Archive Photos (Robert Schumann);

The Kobal Collection (*Picnic at Hanging Rock*);

Pictorial Press Limited (*Blackboard Jungle*);

Australian Picture Library/Redferns/D. Redferns (Bill Haley and the Comets);

The Glenn A Baker Archives (Elvis Presley);

The Kobal Collection (*Hatari!*);

Steve Granitz/Retna (Henry Mancini, © 1993);

Australian Picture Library (Iguaçu Falls);

Performing Arts Library (harpsichord, © Clive Barda);

The Kobal Collection (*Amadeus*);

Archive Photos (Wolfgang Amadeus Mozart);

The Photo Library, Sydney (Earth, Mars and Venus);

Australian Picture Library/Archive Photos (Richard Strauss);

Performing Arts Library (Gyorgy Ligeti, © Clive Barda);

Australian Picture Library/Carnemolla (Johann Strauss);

International Photographic Library (Pig);

Performing Arts Library (Camille Saint-Saëns, © Clive Barda);

Nigel Westlake (photo of himself, photo by John McCormick);

Performing Arts Library (celeste, © Colin Willoughby);

The Kobal Collection (*Batman*);

The Kobal Collection (*Ben Hur*);

The Kobal Collection (*Creature from the Black Lagoon*);

The Kobal Collection (*Henry V*);

Air-Edel Associates (Patrick Doyle);

The Kobal Collection (*Far and Away*);

The Kobal Collection (*Gone with the Wind*);

Australian Picture Library/Bettman (Ludwig von Beethoven);

Motion Picture and Television Photo Archive (*Psycho*);

The Kobal Collection (Alfred Hitchcock);

The Kobal Collection (*Saturday Night Fever*);

The Kobal Collection (*Schindler's List*);

Ronin Films (*Shine*);

The Kobal Collection (*Conan the Barbarian*, © 1981 Dino Delaurentiis Corporation)